On Being Freer

Caleb Gattegno

Educational Solutions Worldwide Inc.

First published in the United States of America in 1975. Reprinted in 1988. Reprinted in 2010.

Author: Caleb Gattegno

ISBN 978-0-87825-085-1

Educational Solutions Worldwide Inc.
2nd Floor 99 University Place, New York, N.Y. 10003-4555
www.EducationalSolutions.com

Table of Contents

Preface

At the age of sixteen I wished I were a free man.

Philosophers were either telling me that I could never be a free man, that such a thing did not exist (because men could not avoid being conditioned and were held down simply by having a body), or they were exalting me (as Epictetus did, by revealing a contempt for whatever bound men to their conditions—thus producing a glimpse of what a free man could be).

Since then I have entertained the notion of being a free man on so many occasions and in connection with so many lightings that I have become clearer about the matter to the point that I am now able to share my understanding of it with others, who may have similar concerns.

In 1942, at the moment of danger presented by Rommel's threat to the Middle East, I read the Bhagavad-Gita. It appeared to me as the song of freedom for my soul, the text from which I could learn how to move towards, and perhaps reach, freedom. As a first contribution to my growth in freedom, it made me see the uselessness of running away from a visible danger only perhaps to run into an invisible one, and I remained calmly where I was—to face myself in the midst of general panic. That summer of 1942 in Cairo brought me the first germs of awareness of what has slowly become the substance of this book.

I understood then that because I existed in time and was mostly unaware of so much that I needed to know to act properly on all occasions, I could hope to be free only by developing a watchfulness of every moment, accumulating and integrating the lessons learned so that the immensity and inevitability of my ignorance would not detract from whatever I had to do to gain a view of what is rather than of what I wished for.

As I progressed through my watchfulness in my immersion in life and living, I saw that although I might never be a "free" man capable of "one free act," I could be freer here and now, and could consciously know the condition of being freer in contrast to that of being lived, the state that so subtly takes away our chances to make genuine choices.

I did not discuss my progress and progression in this field; it was so easy to get lost in words and metaphors. I kept at it, watching myself, questioning what I was doing with myself in the thousands of circumstances of everyday living and what others also engaged in living were doing, in so far as I could grasp it. In all these years I have learned much but neither became a philosopher nor spoke out on freedom, or for freedom. Instead, I became a student of how in our living we create obstacles to being ourselves, obstacles to being connected with what really is, and therefore, I opted to speak only of what I really knew to be true. I did not have to go far to find this out; my life was as good an arena as the best equipped laboratory or university seminar. I looked for places where the automatic work of prejudice could be exposed and perhaps stopped so as to generate a person without that characteristic and I found that such a way of working was fruitful.

Completely dedicated to finding as many obstacles as I could in my own person and life as I could and in attempting to see what I could do to remove them for my own benefit, and since I knew directly what was "better" for me in the circumstances I was satisfied that I was progressing.

This book could have been written as a biography, for I have learned much about myself involved in the acts of living. However, I know that it is not the events of my own life that matter in a study of freedom but what readers can learn for themselves to be able to say: "I am freer today than I was yesterday." Because every one of us has the criteria to make his own decision on this matter of freedom, every one of my readers can tell himself: "Indeed, I am freer."

It is not with the second best of being freer rather than being free that we are concerned here; it is with the only reality. If I can convince my readers of this through the details of working on freeing myself and others of whatever bars us from feeling free here and now in the many different circumstances of our lives, I shall have acted as I want to, that is, as a teacher concerned with growth in awareness. As a teacher my sole aim is to make my students independent, autonomous, and responsible in the precise area under consideration. I have found these characteristics—independence, autonomy, responsibility—to be the instruments of gaining freedom from this or that here and now, so that in the areas where I have educated myself, I am indeed free and knowingly so.

But about the areas where I have not entered, or not entered enough to feel either independent or autonomous and, therefore, not responsible, there is no question of being free and no nostalgia for not being so.

The two areas of being free and of not being free are known to each of us, and while we can say a lot about the first we can say almost nothing of the second. I shall be freer still when I am clear about their coexistence and never forget it.

On the basis of what one has done in one life, has been lucky to do, and knows one has done, the feeling of being freer is not far from the feeling of being free, but it is healthier, because it is more realistic, and, in any case, all that one can be.

In retrospect, that reading of the Bhagavad-Gita in 1942 offered me the fabric of the awareness that I can only be freer and also that I need to be at the task of being freer all the time if I wish to remain in contact with my potential for freedom from all the uses of myself that condition me. This contact may be the source of the concept of freedom, from which indeed I had to be freed before I could know myself as a freer man every minute of my life.

This contact has lasted and is still with me, and as a man who has not lost touch with his process of freeing himself, I am as free a man as I can be. Perhaps in my knowing this I have attained the reality of my sense of freedom in actuality, the actuality of living as it is open to each of us.

The words above were written in 1975. In this revised edition of the work, thirteen years later, I have nothing to add except my thanks to Harris Dienstfrey, who undertook the revision.

Caleb Gattegno

Introduction:
Looking at the Psyche

In my studies of consciousness I came to know my self and some of its workings, which I realized were present from the moment of conception on. It became clear to me that the self is a complex entity that knows itself in time, that is, that the self is capable of knowing more and more of what it is and what it does with time through living.

There was a need to create a new vocabulary every time I met an aspect of the self that had previously been neglected. In particular, the transformation of the energy of the self into forms which, though dynamic, were endowed with an apparent permanence, led me to speak of objectification or objectivation. This, in the realm of biology, is analogous to the process by which physicists view the equivalence of energy and matter in mutual transformation, via Einstein's formula, $E=mc^2$.

The new vocabulary that emerged in my study of the self made it possible to handle complicated questions that were formerly reserved to philosophers and were rarely tackled by scientists. Since 1950 many of my books have been dedicated to the new investigation of such questions and their consequences.*

For the readers of this book a short introduction to the view of psychology contained in these books will be useful.

Energy, Time, and the Work of the Self

I start always with the self, for that is the beginning of the person.

The self that knows that each of us is a person, the same person from babyhood to old age, the self that knows that the muscles respond to its orders and that memory is true—the self that composes songs, pictures, etc.—is also the maker of its own soma, that is, the tissues and organs (including the brain) that begin as an egg and end up at birth as a complex organization meant not only for survival in all sorts of environments but also for learning all sorts of skills over the years.

To understand what is meant by the intrauterine transformation of the self's energy into the soma (the self's first major objectification), we must know that the concept of energy

---

* See the bibliography at the end of the book.

developed by physicists over the last two hundred years permits energy to take forms that are extremely different from one another in appearance but that essentially are one. Heat is so different from electricity, mechanical work from magnetism, and steam power from chemical reactions that physicists themselves took almost a century to accept the essential unity of energy under all these forms.

Using cosmic energy in the form of atoms and molecules and vital energy in the form of cells, the energy of the self produces (in the way that plants and animals do) a cellular edifice that is made of tissues and organs, and is inhabited everywhere by its presence. Since the objectivation of the self in its soma takes place in time and is known in detail to the molecular biologists and the embryologists, we can all know how we have undertaken the job of being in intimate association with our soma every minute of our life and understand why it responds so precisely and immediately to the commands of our <u>will</u> through the functionings of the brain.

Because we draw material from the environment and because DNA is part of the initial cell or egg, there is in our soma an imprint from our habitat and our forebears. Yet because it is the self that undertakes the selection, filtering, sifting, and transforming of the given and the received, each <u>individual</u> human being is a unique system capable not only of having more or less standard behaviors in agreement with the soma but also of having some behaviors that belong strictly to the individual.

We shall call person each individual human being in whom the will is stressed and who is moved all the time by the presence of the will.

It is easy to imagine sap permeating every cell in a tree, and blood running not only through veins and arteries but also through capillaries, thus bathing all the tissues of the living organism of any animal. It is sufficiently easy to conceive that the complex functionings of individual animals and men are coordinated, orchestrated by a nervous system culminating in the brain, which supervises all vegetative life. It may be as easy to imagine that in the process of the in utero transformation of the blood of one's mother into our flesh, there is a dual system of subordinating the already built to the newly built, of integrating the old in the new, all the time producing a more adequate edifice for the dwelling of the self.

At this stage in our brief presentation of what I examine at greater length in a number of my other publications, we must ask our readers to make sure that the model they are developing in their minds is experienced as a dynamic system, closed neither from the past nor to the future. Seeing it in time enables one to maintain the edifice in the making, and to refer to it as it is achieved at every moment between conception and any stage after birth. Only if the component of time is always kept in, will the mental model maintain the throbbing character of life and permit us to consider the various moments of one's life when the conjunction of energy, will, soma, functions, events, etc., affect the reality under consideration.

The Lightings of the Self

Many more things gain relief and are understandable in this dynamic model than can be grasped through models that are based on fragmentation. (My primary handicap in such a discussion comes from the fact that, wanting to use speech to express myself, I necessarily must present the content of my vision in time—that is, as a succession of statements which trigger only at "the end" what I see all at once.) I do not use fragmentation as a method nor do I think that the expansion of my vision over a stretch of time is analysis. Instead, I know that I always hold the whole of the challenge I am contemplating in my <u>intuition</u> so long as I do some things of which I can become aware.

For example, I use the <u>lighting</u> available to myself to produce <u>reliefs</u> in the intuited whole; this process indicates my power to <u>stress</u> some aspects or factors while <u>ignoring</u> the rest. It is stressing and ignoring, which is done in time all the time, that produces the dynamic character of the whole to which one can refer again and again in order to <u>extract</u> new material—previously ignored "stuff" that can now alter appreciably what has been singled out.

Through this approach, no problem is ever closed, and no two moments produce the same yield. Everything is revisable and alterable simply because the whole is known in detail via changeable lightings and is never totally equivalent to the inventory already produced.

My person extended over the time of my life is the subject of my self's attention, and the revealed person is always less than the whole person available in the various edifices that the self can erect and to which it has access through awareness.* My person is simultaneously somatic, intellectual, social, mystical, to name a few attributes; moreover, it carries this complex of qualities all the time.

The Self's Three Forms of Energy

Here we want to bring to the fore the yield that a particular lighting makes possible. Dwelling on the energy aspect of the self, we see that at every moment the self consists of three kinds of energy discernible through awareness. One kind we shall call locked up energy: it is found in objectivations, and it needs to remain in them once the self has decided that it should. This part of the self's energy is for all intents and purposes irretrievable, hence the term locked up.

Another kind of energy we shall call residual energy. This is the energy left by the self to relate the objectivations to one another and to the self via systems of functions. This residual energy is labile but not loose. It is under the supervision of the self and transferred from place to place to perform jobs which are required, in particular, to meet events that surprise one. Blushing is one of the manifestations of residual energy, and we

* See my study, The Mind Teaches the Brain.

know that although blushing is a biological behavior, it is caused by social triggers.

A third kind of energy we shall call free energy. At every stage of the self's construction of edifices, it knows itself as free energy and knows that the awareness of the workings of the will is the contact the self has with free energy. In our life in utero, in our early childhood, we are deeply aware of that free energy and use it normally to cope with the immense unknown surrounding us.

The self on a multitude of occasions and at different levels delegates its authority to some part or aspect of itself. Everyone knows, for example, that the brain seems to be in command of so many somatic functions that in the West—with the so-called "scientific method"—it is rare to find a biologist who acknowledges any entity beyond the brain. Yet other civilizations, as advanced as or more advanced than the West in a number of fields, have studied the self without much reference to the brain. Their methods enabled the people in these civilizations to know physiological functionings without reference to anatomy and to educate themselves in ways not understandable to Western scientists.

Once we begin, as we have here, with energy, taking from certain non-Western civilizations their ways of treating energy, we can reconcile the findings of all serious schools of biology and psychology over the past millennia.

The free energy of the self is energy aware of itself. It is always possible to call for free energy to assist residual energy in its work; it is always possible for residual energy to assist locked up energy to dynamize the objectivations in some way. This is so because everything is integrated in the self, which ultimately decides what to do with its energy at particular moments.

Maintaining the Old, Meeting the New

We shall distinguish two opposite uses of residual energy. When it is mobilized to cope with the demands of the immediate future, we shall call it affectivity; when it is mobilized to cope with the demands of the past, we shall call it psyche.

Affectivity by definition will not be connected with memory, whereas the psyche will dwell in it, and dwells also in many other somatic functionings. Affectivity and the psyche are two aspects of the self back to back, so to speak—very close and very far apart at the same time.

We would not have needed two terms if it had not been found that in the complexity of living, the self is simultaneously involved here and now with the impact of the past and the opening of the future.

The psyche in contact with the soma constitutes the temperament of a person. The soma brings to this unit the "stable" part, and the psyche brings the "labile" part. When some molecular component in the edifice of the soma seems to play a particular role, we can perceive that temperaments could be systematically connected with certain atoms (as is maintained, for example, by homeopathy). Temperaments are seen sometimes as predominantly somatic, sometimes as predominantly psychic. Hinduism proposes three constellations of behaviors: the sattvic, with a minimal influence of the locked up energy on the residual; the rajassic, with a maximal influence; and, in between, the tamassic, with undecided dominance for all cases. The sattvic can more easily take flights of the spirit than the rajassic, who is deeply mixed up with the chemistry of life and more down to Earth. The tamassic, according to his "moods," resembles one or the other of the extremes.

Leaving aside this (heavily loaded) Indian philosophy, we can see already that there is much to describe when we consider how residual energy is connected to the locked up energy of the objectified self. Much has been written on the psyche, mainly by (so-called) depth psychologists, but there still remains a great deal more to understand—and it needs to be treated neutrally, without biases, or at least by stating the biases clearly so as to reduce confusion.

By introducing two aspects of the self, one working with the objectified past (the psyche) and one working on the future (affectivity), the present is accounted for by the self itself, because it integrates all the functionings needed to cope with the challenges encountered. So both the psyche and affectivity will be found at work every moment. As time passes, the role of the psyche distinguishes itself more and more from that of affectivity simply because there is more that is objectified, soliciting the automatic uses of the self, while affectivity can remain the same and always cope with the immediate future.

Change and the Psyche

Since the psyche is called in more and more often to mobilize the part of the past that is needed to meet present challenges, the self can easily find in the automatization of functionings the criteria for becoming free for new tasks, that is, it can delegate to the psyche more and more tasks, which then become unconscious and subconscious. Hence, the psyche is rightly seen as intimately connected with the subconscious and the energy in it. If, because of this, the psyche appears capable of fooling the self and of pulling strings and guiding the lives of at least those patients studied by psychiatrists and psychologists, it does not in truth subordinate the self to part of it. Only so long as the self has no reason to question the way it has delegated its powers and has not found the need to intervene, will the workings of the psyche dominate. But because the self is actually in command, because the psyche is only one aspect of the self, it is possible to call in affectivity and intelligence to transform the energy content of psychic movements, to return the self to its rightful place at the helm, and thus allow it to use the will to put new functionings in the place of others.

In our model, intelligence is the movement of the self mobilizing energy. It can be psychic intelligence, which keeps things as they are, or affective intelligence, which makes possible the introduction of a change. Both intelligences mobilize past capabilities, but while the widening of functionings called in by the psyche for the encounter with the present leaves some components untouched and the psychic status quo intact, the similar widening called in by affectivity changes the status quo. It seems that when a change is required in the use of one's energy, psychic intelligence acts as if it is not very intelligent at all (I call it stupid intelligence), while intelligent intelligence copes with the challenge by turning to affectivity, which is linked to the future and to conscious living.

That the psyche wants to perpetuate the status quo results (1) from it being by definition, insufficient energy that is residually left behind to maintain contact with the past and (2) from the value of automatic functionings, which are solicited all the time to cope with the future and which need to be free for that.

The psyche—being energy and not objectivations—can find itself in contact with the soma as if it, the psyche, were in command. There are many occasions during the day when the self recognizes that the psyche is doing its job well and deserves to be left alone to do what it has been created to control. Only when the working of the psyche is checked by the self (which can call in any one of the other components of itself to achieve ends that it proposes consciously in its contact with actuality) can residual energy affect any change in the use of objectified energy. Affectivity and intelligence cooperate and release some workings from the unity, soma-psyche, so that they can recast themselves in a new unit where the self is present and in command. Change can take place and be judged for what it is—adequate or not for coping with the challenge. If it is not adequate, a renewed intervention of the self is needed; the self must replace the psyche in the field in question and remain the controller as long as needed.

What affectivity does in such cases is to bring in fresh residual energy to activate parts of the organized self that are latent in the soma but are not involved by the psyche in the present meeting of challenges. Affectivity can do the same work as the psyche, but it operates only momentarily to force open a psychic gate or to reorganize energy within the objectified. It then cedes its place to an enlarged psyche, which now holds more than it did before and functions again as it did before but with the consciousness of an altered basis. Automatic functioning is still needed so that the self can be free to cope with the unknown, but by altering the content of the automatic part, some tasks which were impossible earlier can now become easy and second nature.

New Behavior

When the self is moved to intervene in what has been organized, the psyche may propose resistances and argue with the self for the status quo. If the self is determined for its own reasons to obtain a change, it must then bring about the dissolution of resistances and oppositions. Affectivity is needed for this job since it not only works like the psyche, as residual energy closely in contact with all the objectified, but also is aware of itself as being available and not mortgaged to the past. Affectivity must be mobilized to propose the amounts of energy to block temporarily some automatic functionings and to nourish the movements toward new and different behaviors.

Any change of behavior involves the will, and hence the work appears as a struggle to dislodge the psyche from its occupations of some territory mistakenly abandoned by the self.

If the self does not maintain its access to both the psyche and affectivity simultaneously, it has to be called in to work on the psyche and forgo its freedom. This is clearly the case for a number of human beings, particularly "mental patients," who need much more than affectivity to put their house in order. While this operation is going on, the self is aware that all its attention is given to working on the past, that it is inhibited from doing what is properly human—entering the future. Still, only affectivity, as the aspect of the self in contact with the objectified, can do the remedial work—helped by intelligence and the establishment of a special feedback mechanism that evaluates the change as it takes place.

Profound changes cost more than other changes in terms of energy and time taken away from human living, but both kinds of changes are brought about by the same working of human energy. This must be understood by those who want to alter habits which are as innocuous as tooth brushing, or as heavy as drinking. In both cases the intervention of the self is needed to extract the energy given over to the automatic behavior. The watchfulness of the self is passed on to affectivity to mobilize enough energy to alter one's behavior as soon as one is engaged in the activity or on the verge of it. Only the self can become aware that the habit, which works automatically, can be intervened with; only the self, via the psyche, knows what parts of itself have been subtracted from its vigilance and put under the control of the psyche (which may cause warning signs to be ignored or cause the person to be engulfed in habits with no feedback reaching the self). The psyche may point to an appetite, say, as a justification for maintaining the functioning that a habit is. So, living at the automatic level via the psyche the person does not suspect that anything can be done to come out of it and therefore remains in the state of the status quo with regard to harmful behaviors.

But once alerted, the self can delegate to affectivity—which can at any time be in contact with the same objectified realm as the psyche—the job of pouring enough energy into a behavior to alter it and to note the alteration. When the past no longer immediately commands that one yields to the strength of the automatic but rather that one yields to a future envisioned by the self as an expression of itself, the role of affectivity is to inject energy into some mechanisms so that their presence will be felt within the objectified and the new functioning thus has a chance to become as legitimate as other functionings of the self. Then, within the person, the dynamics of the self begins a complex work of temporarily maintaining the intervention of affectivity and of withdrawing from the psyche energy that had been sunken into the habit. The result, of course, is a changed behavior. Sustained by affectivity so long as hope is present—and this represents the future—the new functioning and its expression in behaviors is now under the scrutiny of the self. When the new functioning is considered safe, it is passed to the care of the psyche, and it becomes a thing of the past, freeing the self for other jobs yet to come.

In the realm of habits, we can see at once how all this is at work. In the various chapters of Part I we shall handle the details of how we learn to free ourselves of psychic dominances.

The Psyche and the Ego

Another functioning of the psyche is concerned with adherences. Excessive energy can be given to psychic movements and kept there for some time. We shall call ego the psychic structures that have this excess of energy. The ego is part of the psyche, hence of the self, but because of the adherences it weighs more than is needed, though its content resembles the rest of the psyche. Ego movements occupy more space than other psychic movements. For example, language is a psychic functioning and works by itself smoothly and well, but the content of statements made in that language may well be ego statements, excessively concerned with the personality of the speaker, a distorted image of himself being at the root of the selection of the content carried by the language.

The psyche may produce the ego and egocentric movements because the self has not given itself the necessary vigilant components to watch over its functioning. Producing such components remains the privilege of the self, but they are not necessarily produced in every case and all circumstances.

The self, through its will and its sense of truth, can keep the psyche in check and can prevent the formation of an overgrown ego. Such supervision of the psyche by the self is part of the mental health of each person, but in the struggles for survival in nature and society not everyone recognizes that such supervision has first priority. So most people end up having too much ego—that is, more adherences than are needed to steer one's way in the world—and also a psyche that deludes them and plays them against their real best interest.

The Separate Tasks of Psyche and Affectivity

Let it be understood that the psyche is not a villain, nor is affectivity an angel; both are needed equally by the self to carry on the jobs of the inner life in conjunction with the objectified. Only when they engage in a dynamic reversal of what already is automatic in the objectified do they have opposite functionings: one pulls for the status quo (the psyche); the other for an altered behavior (affectivity).

So long as no functioning is put in question, the self sees affectivity and the psyche as parts of itself, both available as surplus energy in contact with the objectified, and the self treats them as channels to its past. But as soon as the question of altering behavior is put, both become different, and it is possible to see why both need to be given different functions in the overall maintenance of life for survival.

For readers of this book, the central theme in all subsequent chapters will be how to engage more consciously in handling affectivity as the changer and the psyche as the rules of the automatic. Every one of the chapters will illustrate in detail how we can stop being lived—if we prefer to live instead.

Relating to Others

What we have written above places the self in contact with the objectified self in terms of two functions represented by the psyche and affectivity. If we relate to others, the energy of both functions can be noted from outside, and it becomes possible for one person to find his self or any of its components affected by the state of energy in another person.

A new realm opens up for people who find it worth their while to specialize in the impacts of psyches upon one another.

It is even possible to develop a number of functionings of the self in this realm and to act as a scout or a radar system, becoming more easily affected by the affective and psychic tones of others, reaching sometimes very finely tuned states that serve as antennae in human relations.

A specialist in this realm can either remain an investigator or become active. In the first case, the information received may be collected for no end or for specific ends, of which study is one; in the second case, the developed capabilities can serve in one or more professions—medicine, law, politics, education—to provide access to others in order to heal them, serve them, or exploit them.

For such people, psychic movements are as visible as behaviors. Direct access to the movements of psyches is as much an instrument as a weapon; it will depend on the ethic of the person to do what he will with such power over others.

Such access, coupled with a dedication to other people's "good," may lead to the assistance many need.

Part I

On Becoming Freer

1 From Jealousy

I cannot say when I first experienced jealousy, but I remember when I knew it to be the experience called by that name because at that time I also experienced the need to look into it.

What came to me was that I was in contact with <u>inner</u> material: with emotions and their dynamic, and with access to both as well as to the feeling of pain and confusion that accompanied jealousy.

I had read about jealousy; I had heard people talk about it, in regard to themselves and to others. But while it remained either remote or not too deep, I remember in my adolescence saying to myself only, "You are jealous," and not pursuing it further. I also remember seeing that it had attributes that made me view it as synonymous with possessiveness. Not once then did I judge that it was not justified or legitimate, mainly because it expressed love.

Years of confusion about what it actually was, and how I could cope with it, followed. It is not possible to retrace the road I took, but I can say that I have known jealousy and still know what it was, for today I am almost completely free of it.

I suspect that most of my readers know of jealousy. Though I cannot speak on their behalf, I can pursue the study of jealousy on everyone's behalf by considering my own examination of jealousy, minus the details of the specific circumstances, and thus make it possible for others to use their personal experiences.

The first illusion concerning jealousy that I noticed was that I believed jealousy was caused by one or two outsiders, not by myself. That illusion could last as long as these outsiders were in my field of attention. It was so obvious to me that the trigger of jealousy came from somewhere other than myself and that when this outside trigger did not exist I did not feel jealous. So I absolved myself at once and put the blame on the outsiders.

This is precisely the mechanism that makes us pursue an inner status quo and keeps us in the same track and prevents us from working on what removes jealousy.

In my case, since I was a student of myself and interested in not being fooled, every occasion in which I found myself jealous was both lived intensely and considered by a watchful self. By living it intensely, I knew that I was a jealous person who gave himself the right to be so and justified himself in the steps he took in relation to jealousy. The arguments that presented themselves, as justifying jealousy, were unilateral but I did not feel them to be biased. On the contrary, for a while interest in, love of, another person automatically triggered the concomitant inner movement which denied that person a freedom of being that clearly existed before my expression of interest or love.

This point, faintly perceived at first, gained significance and assisted me in understanding the working of jealousy and in finally gaining freedom from it.

There is nothing intellectual in the movement away from jealousy; the intellect is mightily impotent in handling it. It is even possible that the intellect only adds its clumsiness to the difficult job of coping with the dynamics of an energy that, in jealousy, comes in considerable amounts. *If there is a golden rule in the struggle to understand jealousy, it is to stop thinking of it and do very different things instead.*

Jealousy is not a given. When Freud sees it as an aspect of the dynamics of the subconscious and gives it the name of Oedipus complex, he is telling us only of a methodological device which may or may not be appropriate in all cases. More often than not, loving fathers are not considered as competitive by babies; clumsy fathers and dismissive fathers, however, may draw attention to what will be one day be fixated as jealousy in his children.

Possessiveness, unlike jealousy, is a given—and is a more broadly based phenomenon. It can be the expression of our relationship with anything we need to be linked to (even as babies) to acquire a particular learning. For example, when we learn to grasp, we seek objects that provide a variety of experiences, and as long as we have something to investigate with these objects, we resent anyone removing them from our reach. Possessiveness in such cases is biological, and serves real and valuable purposes, but it may turn itself into an ego functioning and generate adherences to objects after they have fulfilled their function. Once such attitudes are formed, the individual finds himself believing that to express possession is biological, instinctual, legitimate. Those among us for whom this is the case find it strange that such attitudes be questioned.

When a given environment—a home or a family group within a home—supports the movement of possessiveness on the part of some of its members, the expansion from things to people can take place. Exaggerated attachments make possessiveness into a rule, and possessiveness can change into jealousy as soon as circumstances hint at a threat to one's "ownership" of another person.

Such examples show how jealousy grows out of possessiveness that has been allowed to extend itself from objects to people and how jealousy is regarded by the jealous person as a legitimate response which offers no reason to engage in its elimination or even diminution. Such jealous persons continue forever to act as though they were victims of the interference of people who want what is theirs. Sometimes they are hurt because the person they think is theirs cooperates with the intruder. In such cases, it is possible that the stress produced by the circumstances may awaken the jealous person to <u>his</u> trespasses and may begin in him a movement of self-education capable of freeing that person from the intensity of righteous indignation that nourishes jealousy.

In communities where ownership is not stressed, the feeling of jealousy exists, but the alert self can put things right by taking some inner steps.

It is conceivable that a society could exist in which everyone, watching the movements of the self, encourages only those moves acceptable to all and therefore avoids the trespass leading to jealousy.

But outside such a society, we find people who are mentally equipped with both a certain possessiveness and the processes that justify the feeling on "moral" grounds.

To free ourselves from such an entanglement we have only the functionings of the self itself.

As in all freeing movements, we find here that it takes time. Even for those who work well, time is needed; this is due to the fact that we have to do an existential job requiring precise circumstances that may not present themselves continuously, or even when we are ready to work on them. Because it will take time to become freer of jealousy, we must work on it every time it presents itself and seek to make some progress. Each of us alone can answer the question of progress. We therefore need to develop criteria that tells us we are getting better at recognizing that we are more aware of jealousy when it is triggered, or that we can develop in us the watchfulness that keeps us in contact with our jealous movements and the justifying mechanisms we develop to keep ourselves in that track, or that we are more capable of bringing to the center of our consciousness the arguments that weigh on behalf of others so as to tilt the balance toward their side and heed them more and more, or that we can develop devices that add a moderation to the situation, such as: "What would happen if I were absent?" or "What would happen if I were in the other's place?" and similar relativistic criteria.

Of course, each of us will have to devise the approach to our own unique manifestation of jealousy and foster the moves that yield a greater awareness of and a deeper acquaintance with the components accessible to the self. What applies to all of us, however, is that we can be carried away by the symptoms of jealousy, and feeling pain in jealousy, we can trigger a defense mechanism that blurs the issues, affectively and intellectually.

We all prefer to let others take the steps that restore things to the state they were before the intruder (real or imaginary) appeared. This delays our entering into the situation to do something involving ourselves, or even can postpone it forever.

We all prefer to be right and therefore construct an edifice of uncertain affective-cum-intellectual meshes to remove any blame from us and put it squarely on the other.

We all prefer to do what serves to reinforce our image of ourselves, and instead of acknowledging that jealousy can dwell in us, we shift the ground and present ourselves as magnanimous and conciliatory while the wounds caused by our jealousy deny it all.

We all prefer to repeat our experiences of jealousy, shifting from subject to subject or intruder to intruder, always finding in the specificity of the circumstances a uniqueness, rather than meeting in one place—in ourselves—the trigger of jealousy and coping with it. We prefer to look at the outside scenes rather than the inner movements.

We all prefer to glorify the self rather than to work on it with its full cooperation. Perhaps this happens because we have made ourselves much more capable of looking outward and describing what we see, than of letting the self meet itself in direct confrontation with our responsibility for what we do with our self. We may even have lost contact with the self and go so far as to deny that we have one or are one. Glory for one's ego can result from actions that have no bearing on freeing us from jealousy—for example, by dropping altogether our affection for someone, by finding oneself capable of turning one's back on the person we said so recently that we were interested in, by finding oneself ready to abandon a relationship because it is not working according to our desires. These egocentric moves (even if they are not accompanied by a sense of glory for one's ego, they enhance other ego mechanisms) would not touch jealousy, and the presence of pain would indicate to the ego that nothing is working, and jealousy would once again occupy one's consciousness. Because the ego can be flattered, the energy of jealousy can be transferred to the feeling of glory that results from an ego made to feel superior, when in fact the self has been defeated.

We all prefer to live with as little consciousness of our self and our will as possible, to entertain schemas instead of the complex persons in ourselves and others.

But the truth is that we are complex, that relationships are complex, that schemas, if they are easier to manipulate mentally, are useless in actuality, that it does not really help anyone to hide his head in the sand.

The sooner we wake up to this truth, the easier it will be to cope with the movements of the self that thwart our lives.

In our inner life we have not only the unfolding of time lived but also the wealth of the work of the self present from conception; in our inner life we can find what no effort, however great, can bring from outside. Jealousy is one of the moves of our inner life, and it is in this inner life that we find a capacity to meet it, to understand it, to deal with it.

How can we do this?

As much as it is true of the outside world, our inner life is also made up of energy and its manifestations. But while we have studied, over centuries and in detail, how to handle cosmic energy in the cosmos, vital energy on Earth, and animal energy in our domination over nature, we still have to study, in the required scale and forms, the energy of the self.

In our inner life our grossest contact with energy occurs when we find how much of it is mobilized for anger and indignation.

If we pursue the search a little further, we find that energy is available at all moments. Whether we use some to raise our voice to make our sounds reach people at a distance, or to open a tightly closed jar, or to affect our lips when we speak or our fingers when we write, we can recognize that we have in store an amount of energy that can be shifted from tissue to tissue or organ to organ or functioning to functioning (of which we are not yet quite aware). This energy is not felt as palpably in certain circumstances, but we can know it is there— available, at the disposal of our will—as much as it is in other conditionings. We can shift from our awareness of the existence of this energy to awareness of its functioning, and gradually we can become truly acquainted with it and learn to use it for our own ends: ends dictated perhaps by our watchfulness.

Anyone who becomes acquainted with this energy and its movements learns to follow it, to meet it settling into places or in movement from place to place, and such encounters are clearly part of our inner life. Watchfulness of this kind is self awareness—the self awareness that is a power because it is awareness of the self and is not self consciousness.

Knowing that the self can command its energy to be present voluntarily in certain functionings or to be withdrawn voluntarily from where it already is, makes it possible to consider freeing oneself, through some work and discipline—inner work and inner discipline, from what one's watchfulness describes as a dysfunction.

Jealousy is a dysfunction mainly because it is recognized by the individual who lives it (or is lived by it) as painful, undesirable, time consuming, not really justified in existing.

Once the self recognizes in full awareness that jealousy partakes in the working of the psyche and the ego, the movement for freeing oneself from it is possible. Without such awareness all efforts would be vain, since the psyche is able to fool itself and perpetuate its functionings in disguise.

But such awareness is not sufficient. The self has produced the soma and the psyche in time, and some vital links may have been underenergized and therefore may remain inaccessible to one's watchfulness for some time! What took time to become structured energy cannot be undone without peril to the whole self unless one is lucky and strikes at the right places and can easily do the repair work. This repair work, which takes time, also takes energy. Not energy for consumption (this exists but is insignificant) but for the awareness of energy, so that the self can know whether the energy exists in excess or insufficient amounts.

In the case of jealousy, most mechanisms have been overloaded, while a few have been insufficiently supplied. The road to greater freedom lies in correcting this energy distribution. It will take the time it takes to enter into relationship with this dynamic, to learn to recognize the faulty structuring of the psyche, to act upon the free energy in order to withdraw the excesses and supply the insufficiently loaded ones.

Once we know what kind of work there is to do, we are incomparable better equipped than we are when we have no idea that it is we who must free ourselves.

Once we are alerted to the existence of particular dynamics in our inner life, we are already on the road to freedom.

Once we develop the watchfulness of the peculiar dynamics that go to form jealousy and nothing else, we have started the movement of freeing ourselves from it.

To work on jealousy the self must consciously accept its existence and give attention to it as it takes place. The discipline of being with it—of holding the complexity of one's inner life as it actualizes itself here and now—is required. And this too takes time, for the education we give ourselves in our societies rarely calls for it. We are capable of this discipline, but we do not know it because we are generally distracted by looking at other things and hence lose sight of it.

Anyone wanting to cope with jealousy must first manage to respect it, that is, let it be itself within a self now capable of watching it for what it is.

This means (1) that the self is capable of living the events of life, inner and outer; and (2) that the self knows itself as one—although in an episode of jealousy, part of the self's objectified functionings show themselves as the specific manifestations of jealousy even while the non-objectified self surveys, monitors, records the movements within.

Because this describes in fact how we all are—however faintly we may be it—we can all hope to cope with our jealousy.

Awareness without facility may lead to philosophical discourses. Facility is needed in actuality and is acquired by taking the opportunity to give time to one's jealousy so that one acquires the discipline of coping better and better with its dynamics. Facility can only result from facing oneself in the state of jealousy and learning then and there something about its working in oneself.

Once this has been achieved, the rest is less hard, and freedom from jealousy becomes a possible attainment. Indeed, it now becomes a matter of the will intervening in the process of providing the required dosage of energy for the various functionings in contact with the soma and/or the psyche.

At the precise moment when a movement or affectivity or some images or thoughts make their appearance, the self can cut the supply of free energy and start the following functioning: the watchful self sees both what used to happen (and is now made not to happen) and the result of the new energy supply upon one's behaviors.

If such awareness is followed by other awarenesses that confirm that the working is functional and that one is becoming more and more able to cope with the occurrences of jealousy, a facility is established of which the self is aware when it feeds back to itself that the freeing is taking place more and more.

Starving the functionings that sustain jealousy is therefore objectively known and can become a functioning of the self. It is such functionings that need energizing, for they previously have been starved. The energy this new functioning receives makes it perceptible to the other new functionings set up by the self to take care of this aspect of living in the inner life, which can now be more conscious. And more abundant, because the energy uselessly mortgaged to the mobilizations of jealousy is now available to the self for a living more respectful of the truth in Reality.

More aware of our place in other people's lives and of other people's place in ours, we will give each relationship the energy it needs to function without possessiveness and with a sight of the degrees of freedom we all have in the world of actual relating. We shall stop confusing relating with possessing; we shall acknowledge more and more that, in a world which heeds us but little, we can take our own place only if we leave others to occupy theirs and if we give thanks for the gifts we receive by being accepted by others for what we are. Jealousy not only expresses a right we do not have, to restrict other people's lives in ourselves and sometimes in the world, it also destroys our inner balance, the delicate balance of the processing of each moment of relation. It invades other areas of the self and, as is known, leads to some blinding and to much misery.

Jealousy is to be considered as a functioning because it is displayed in somas, in psyches, in societies, and in cultures; but it is, humanly speaking, better described as a dysfunction of a self that has abandoned its position at the apex of inner life and has accepted the functionings of the psyche as if they were all the self was.

Freeing oneself from jealousy is possible and has a significance beyond itself—namely, that the self returns to its position of control, finds itself better equipped to enter relationships without false investments or costly mortgages, and breathes better in the climate of a human spiritual life.

Although we may be only freer and freer from jealousy, the contact of the self with the process of freeing opens up new hopes of perhaps reaching a completely free relating, in which we knowingly come together to live here and now the gift of togetherness.

2 From Greed

Greed is a subtle psychic functioning.

Its source is appetite.

When we consider that we need to be motivated to make a move to eat but that all animals eat because of hunger, we can see how far man has moved from his supposed origins.

Greed can be recognized in many forms besides eating. Every time an appetite moves someone towards getting for himself what is affecting him, there is a possibility for greed to develop.

There is greed for knowledge or for money or for sexual satisfaction at least as much as there is greed for seafood or brands of cheeses; there is greed for recognition and for esteem, for social eminence and professional success; there is greed for flattery and for attention, for authority and for power.

All these greeds are recognized by the self as having one component in common which makes it possible to place them in one class of feelings, despite the multiplicity of appearances. This component is that as soon as the thing that is coveted is gained, it no longer keeps its value, and the mind hankers for something else.

Because greed is subtle we can speak of mind, instead of psyche, for the energy aspect of greed is not its most conspicuous feature.

Nevertheless, because of the movement from expectancy to expectancy, the lived is absorbed by the psyche, and its contribution is annihilated in terms of the fulfillment it could have brought. Hence, the dynamics stay in the background and are rapidly disposed of, so that the self is not informed that any hankering has been satisfied.

Here again we see another example of the deft manner in which our psyche operates, moving the lighting of its attention from one functioning to another.

That the self follows suit is, in fact, our problem.

Presented by the psyche with something to covet, the self mobilizes itself to obtain it. The self and the psyche become one; the stress is on pursuit—like the pursuit of the hunter who shoots down one bird after another without regard for what is to be done with the prey. The self uses the past while the psyche does all it can so that parts of itself, which could be linked, are prevented from affecting one another. The self is then freed to concentrate upon achieving the end as best it can, and in this there is intrinsic satisfaction. The self knows itself as performing its function: using all that has been organized, all that has been vitalized in the realm of the objectified to achieve an always higher performance.

If there were not a disrespect for what has been gained and a concentration upon another end for one's actions, how could we renew ourselves to eat more, to drink more than our fill, to fornicate once more, to hanker for one more flattering remark, and on and on, without being alerted and becoming conscious of a dysfunction of our psyche?

Greed may become connected with other behaviors that can awaken the self to its duty of keeping its life running smoothly. It is possible that the cynic may question in our presence some of the behaviors by which we hide greed from our awareness. It is possible that a pain, or simply a small accident caused by some clumsiness accompanying one of our activities, may force us to stop and consider what we are doing and lead us to take some initiative to become concerned with our dysfunctions.

Once the self is moved to intervene, it is then possible to enter upon the recognition of what to do to release oneself from the repetitive movements of the psyche which immediately after an action points to another action instead of to the result of the former one.

Like everyone else, I have met many greedy people in my life and of course was greedy myself, thus knowing greed both first hand and by proxy. On more than one occasion, I was struck by the fact that I could notice greed in others before I could find it in myself. I have been told of the "decadent" behavior of Romans in their orgies and could not bring myself to emulate that. But I took part in contests that seemed to me very different because of the competitive element in them, and I would try to eat as many pieces of a certain Greek sweet as I was able to in a given time, satisfied that I could do better next time. I found it normal to stop at a pastry shop at any hour of the day and treat myself without any appetite beyond what greed could develop in me.

One day the act of eating sixteen large bananas, one after the other, gave me such an intestinal condition that for six months I had to eat one and the same tasteless dish (I cannot say whether the doctor who prescribed it was educating me or curing me!).

From then on I changed my sight for food and avoided all excesses; I controlled my greed for "good" things to eat and marveled at neighbors ready to travel 200 miles each way to eat a special dish whose cook had a great reputation. But there was not much evidence in me of a transfer of awareness from greed for food to greed for, say, recognition or knowledge.

I often asked myself whether my thirst for knowledge was greed—was really greed or something else.

Of course, with my growing erudition, with an ease in quoting and in shining among those who appreciated scholarship, I felt knowledge was a quality I was developing, and I indulged in it immoderately. The feedback from the public was all positive; I was singled out as a model for those who wanted their children to shine socially.

One day I was made to see more clearly that I was being moved by greed rather than by a facility to retain what I had encountered because of my good memory. When I discovered a municipal library near my home and visited it to see what it could offer me for my studies, I went in with an enormous appetite. At once I said to myself that I would study all those books on the shelves, that a seventeen-volume encyclopedia could be digested in as many months, that the sciences, the law, literature, linguistics, architecture, history, etc., were all at hand and should be ingested.

A few months later a simple calculation showed me that I needed several lifetimes in that building to achieve an aim which, in retrospect, was not even worthwhile, simply because knowledge becomes obsolete in so many areas.

I still find lingering in me today a thirst for knowledge, but I do not let my psyche persuade me that it can be quenched, and I attempt to read only what is significant to me.

The importance of this personal example is that it showed me how a simple arithmetical operation, which my intelligence put to my self, could reduce a greed from enormity to a reasonable size. The event told me that perhaps the greed harbored within me could be searched, found, and dealt with, and that perhaps it was possible to live an abundant life without any greed to speak of.

What I found that is of value to all is the mechanism of greed: the psyche's fooling of the self, although they are one and the self is in command. I had repeated the view of moralists, that excess in any direction is bad and is to be avoided; and I had recognized in my flesh what excesses were. But I found them attractive and inviting. I found myself willingly following the seductive proposals of my psyche and read in great books that some attractive characters were great because they yielded to excesses.

When I realized that my appetite was not necessarily my ally, I began to watch its working in a number of areas. Food and gastronomy were the easiest to consider, and I became frugal soon after. I was therefore able to insert a wedge between a psychic mechanism triggered by the sight of food and the initiative of the self to command physically possible actions. I had responded automatically to the availability of food by eating; now I could leave it where it was, as it was. I had become free from one tendency that I had encouraged earlier, the greed most accepted because it is associated (wrongly, it seems to me) with the preservation of the individual and the species.

Warned by these two experiences that greed was not a necessary expression of my humanity, I examined its manifestation in a number of other fields.

Balzac and Zola, Dostoevsky and Cervantes, and many other able students of the foibles of mankind served me by illuminating within the vast spectrum of human behavior the role greed plays as a lever for behaviors I would prefer to avoid.

The scene in The Idiot in which a high-value banknote is thrown into the fire, marked me forever. So did the difficulties of the Baron Hulot in La Cousine Bette, or the affairs of the Rongon Macquart family, characters of Zola's artful creation, because of their general inability to handle their various greeds.

Love is often associated with greed, particularly the type called love-attachment. While theoretically the loved ones are to be given the space in us to be themselves, our greed, manifested as possession and possessiveness, often makes things go sour. The need to have the beloved at one's beck and call reduces his or her actual freedom of movement. Greed breeds jealousy.

Some people develop a way of living on the psyche of others. Their greed consists of being occupied and preoccupied with the needs of others, so that as long as they receive satisfaction by being exploited, they are happy. A threat to their greed—by not giving them, for example, the calls for service that correspond to a good level of exploitation— makes them miserable and sometimes sick. This greed is masochistic and almost impossible to reduce, since the person displaying it seems unable to become aware of its existence and significance.

Once again we find that a particular awareness must be present for a freeing process to start. As long as greed is subconscious, it will remain forever as it is. And there are many reasons for it to disappear from one's consciousness: one is that some greeds are not only tolerated in some communities but openly supported as biologically, sociologically, and psychologically valuable; another is that an appetite does not need to attain excessive dimensions to become greed and affect one's personality and one's actual living. It may not be noticeable and yet still be there, like abscesses in our mouths or organs. One more reason is that greed can be disguised as something socially valuable or of merit. For instance, love of money in commercial societies is not counted as greed but as legitimate motivation for doing the right thing in business; accumulation of wealth likewise, even in non-commercial societies.

The greed for approval, so prevalent in the world, is one of the distorters of everyday life that affects most of our societies, even though it sounds innocuous. Not trained at home and school to have inner criteria in areas where they actually exist, most people act with only one outside criterion in mind: approval from others. Every day, in many activities, the self accepts as normal what would be intolerable to a responsible self at work, and it merges with the psyche in (1) waiting for approval before taking further steps and (2) making approval a prerequisite for happiness.

To free a person from this calamitous situation, the self, with the help of wiser selves if they are available, must act on its expectations, starving them one by one while generating inner criteria where they exist, and must receive feedback from reality rather than from people. It is a long but not impossible road; the lessons learned on traveling it may extend beyond the limited scope of each exercise and help the self to become freer more rapidly in other areas of behaviors as well. (If I were to give assistance in this area, it would be by providing exercises in which the self concentrates on finding the criteria that make a person capable of approving, so that one becomes the approving master as well as the expectant apprentice.)

Greed has always been considered by wise people as something to get rid of. Those who managed it did not tell us how they did it. Today we can be clearer on these matters because we look at ourselves as evolving systems endowed with awareness and the capacity for self-education. Greed is one more of the psyche's functionings that illustrate that what can be justified in animals, who are lived by their instinct, becomes a dysfunction in man, who is endowed with a will to alter behaviors. What moralists condemn a priori as an excess that should be corrected, the scientist objectively studying the self looks upon as an existing behavior, which is real because it exists but which may not be not necessary if the self is in control. When excesses are seen in terms of actual techniques to restore balances instead of predetermined codes of behavior, it becomes clear that neither a miracle nor a formula puts things in their place. Rather, as soon as the existential aspect of greed is understood, there follows the understanding of the psyche's functions within the self which dictates a successful way of meeting challenges (except in cases complicated by extraneous circumstances).

Man is neither greedy in essence nor not greedy for any intrinsic reason—the size of his brain, say, or his civilized existence. He becomes greedy by pursuing a bent that attracts him. By letting himself be put on an incline, he yields to forces that live in him, until such a time that he knows himself as utterly redeemable if he uses his endowments of will, intelligence, awareness, and patience to see the appropriate exercises through.

Man knows himself as less greedy if he has done these things often. This is equivalent to freeing oneself more and more from that form of psychic dominance over the self.

3 From Lust

For so many generations men and women have worshipped pleasure and have known that one of its peaks is found in orgasm and the approach of it.

Lust is the label given to the involvement of the psyche in the sexual production of pleasure, and rare are those who do not pursue it.

Moralists consider themselves entitled to approve or condemn; scientists are concerned with facts and with debunking pseudo-facts by pointing at the truth.

Students of sexuality in the animal kingdom have many tales to tell about the competition of males to obtain the favors of a female and the apparel the males have developed to attract her attention. They tell us how the sexual functions in animals are subordinated to reproduction and that rarely do animals undertake sexual intercourse for the pleasure it gives. Animals, it seems, are lived by some pre-established mechanism and mate only in given circumstances. They do not seem to be moved by the "pleasure principle."

Still, some of us may have seen examples of animal sexual intercourse in which the experience had a temporal repercussion at least in the female, who could use her propriosensory system to prolong a sensation she had lived through and was continuing, in so far as the semen deposited by the male was perceptible to her as a foreign body. As for the male, who can deny him access to the memory track immediately following erection and ejaculation?

We can concede that animals engaged in a life much more organized than that of modern urban existence, with a sexual life that is not independent of reproduction—that is, one triggered by a biological mechanism dependent on the most favorable chances of making sperm and ovum meet—have little penchant for separating sexual intercourse from the act of fertilizing the female. But we cannot exclude the possibility that, if circumstances are right, male or female animals may notice what is happening to them and seek its repetition.

Years ago I had a female dog who lived entirely indoors in our city apartment until she ran away. She had been given to us as a very young puppy, and I was accepted as her master because I agreed to clean her excretions. A few months later, and for a few days in a row, in successive months, she used to hold one of my legs between her front paws and furiously move her body in a way that later I could only consider to be masturbation without contact. (Some women masturbate without touching themselves, simply by closing their thighs tightly and moving their outer labia to rub against a protracted clitoris.)

Pleasure was obviously accompanying my dog Joujou's explorations, and the repetition of the act, several times in one sitting, several times in a few days every month, for a few months before she ran away, told me that she at least knew what lust was and was given to it.

In spite of that there may be good reasons for reserving the term lust to mankind.

Indeed, love is one of the prominent components of human living, and love and lust seem closely interrelated but, also, quite easily separable, as all those who masturbate know.

The human problem arises when actions performed by an individual are not acceptable to him or when pressure is exercised from outside (directly or virtually, by delegation) to ban these actions.

Lust may well be a key issue for understanding a large area of human involvement from the viewpoint of consciousness and freedom of the self. We may also in passing discover the main tenets of human sexual education.

Contrary to what happens with jealousy and greed, lust is not bred in early childhood; it becomes truly active only around puberty, which may happen for some as late as their fifteenth year.

Our sight can accept nudity with no special response for years, and then suddenly one day it gains a connotation that transforms the act of seeing. For years our skin was capable of recording the impacts of touches, but one day just as suddenly it develops a resonance that generates echoes, giving to touch an element that prolongs the sensation, exalts it, and magnifies it.

We are concerned here with a learning that does not involve the past; in fact, in the past there were only sketches of what in puberty becomes full-fledged features of the soma. The psyche, in so far as it may have been linked to this somatic feature, would have behaved as innocently in regard to it as it had with all aspects of perception in early childhood. It is this innocence that gives to so much of early childhood experience a matter-of-fact character that is not emotionally disturbing.

But the self has developed its own instruments to meet the simultaneous triple impacts of past, present, and future. When changes in physiology are taking place, it is affectivity that is called in to do the energizing required to cope with the descending unknown. Hence the lability of young adolescents, who have nowhere to turn to apprehend or comprehend what is happening to them in their inner life and in their slowly transforming soma. They use affectivity to try to come to terms with their changing lives.

Outsiders need to be confronted with visible signs in order to be alerted to the existence of a change. Not so for the subject himself, who is well equipped to monitor and survey what is happening within. The self is in its element when it works on the unknown and uses its instruments to come closer to what is required of it in all places: adjusting to the chemical changes occurring; noting the concomitant alterations of size, proportion, complexion; and adjusting to the maintenance of old forms in the mind and in the psyche, some of which are still valid because of functions that need to be continued and others, though still working because of the momentum that accompanies them in everyday living, need to be stopped to prevent interference with growth.

Over the years, the self has seen the psyche as an ally in taking over the jobs tested and found to function well, that is, to the self's satisfaction. Now, in adolescence, the self can intervene only in a delayed manner and finds that affectivity is its true ally and that the psyche must be put in a state of waiting and passivity.

Elsewhere I have made a study of adolescence in its complexity.*
Here, while maintaining contact with this complexity, I want to restrict the area to the title of this chapter: lust, which is born during adolescence and given enough attention then to flourish.

Some readers may find that the example given below to describe the working of the self does not accord with the actual movements in their own lives. Such readers can ask themselves questions similar to the ones handled here and thereby find

---

* See The Adolescent and His Will, 1971.

their own answers rather than consider the description as false simply because it does not apply to them.

If it is true that not all adolescents masturbate, it is also true that not all girls develop large breasts, that not all boys have the same relationship to their genitals. If we consider masturbation, our study concerns those who know it; if we consider feminine appearances, the relationship to one's breasts matters more for those who are not satisfied with what they find is their lot than for those at peace with theirs; if we consider penises per se, what is there that involves some but not others?

The approach we use is one that maintains contact with the whole and, through a number of lightings, illumines first one component, then another, then both together.

The whole is that person facing the onrush of new challenges—that person having a past and extending the present by deliberate involvements in contact with the future seen as the premonition of changes that are occurring.

The lightings may be of various qualities; dim or intense, broad or sharply pointed, intermittent or continuous, in isolation or in conjunction.

The first lighting we used was capable of taking care of the psyche: it seems to be made passive in adolescence because its functions are not needed then. Hence the self can refrain from sending some of its energy to enhance the residual energy necessary to keep some functionings monitored and working well. Instead the self will operate via affectivity, by holding the contact with the newly formed as long as is necessary for awareness to reach it and make some notes about it. Affectivity will temporarily coagulate the residual energy required to produce a transient objectivation which can survey instruments of the self that belong to the psyche, for it is the psyche that informs the self that such a coagulation is either in agreement with existing functionings (to the point of generating the feedback of pleasure) or in conflict with them (with a feedback of pain). Pleasure and pain are old psychic acquaintances and are put into circulation because affectivity remains in contact with the functions of the objectified self, and the psyche is triggered when an old functioning is energized.

Sexual parts, which include so many somatic components—hands, mouths, breasts, genitals—are at first randomly energized, and the echoes are noted. These echoes are part of the psyche by definition and can be retained in one's memory, evoked as images or as residual energy.

As the self becomes more interested in these particular coagulations of energy, it shifts part of its attention, the part related to the echoes, to the psyche. Affectivity withdraws the energy from one coagulation and places it in another, making the first disappear but without erasing its track because it is now a psychic form capable of being re-energized by the psyche. As a psychic form it seems to have only a psychic existence. The same fate applies to the next coagulation of energy, and so on.

Hence, affectivity serves to furnish the psyche with new forms that could not be produced by sheer psychic functioning alone. It still energizes only what it selects, and the results may not require much change in the relationship of psyche and affectivity. Only when enough new material has been created by the self through affectivity to make the psyche note how the soma is affected and that new psychic functionings are being integrated in the self, will the person know he has changed and involve himself in the change—for example, through masturbation, which is a new acquaintance and one of the self's possible functionings. Something new has come one's way. The somatic elements existed from the start; their form was known, but the superficial anatomical examinations undertaken much earlier for sheer curiosity left few echoes. There was so little to know that it was known at once. Even the impact of looking at mating animals or accidentally seeing people in sexual intercourse may not go beyond the visual and the ensuing intellectual acquaintance.

But now, in adolescence, the concomitant hormonic flow is affecting every cell in the soma. The composition of the blood having changed, the soma and the psyche will find that instead of just impacts there are now states lasting long enough for a dialogue to take place. Not only is everything taking place within one's soma, the change is accessible to the scrutiny of the self. The rush of blood which causes the male erection, producing a change not only visible but difficult to hide, is experienced everywhere in that person because it takes place in the self first and in the penis second. Such a rush of blood in the female does not show itself in as visible a manner, but it can be noted in the erection of the nipples and the clitoris. Both male and female are guided from within to the phenomenon and can note that it attracts the self so that the self concentrates itself on and in the changes. To know these changes as produced within oneself, by oneself, there is no further need than to let the echo of the phenomenon trigger the desired change. So no invitation to touch oneself is yet required. The inner movement may be sufficient for someone to know himself or herself as functioning in this new way and to be content with that knowledge. This is a more subtle relationship with oneself than will be needed later to state, "I know myself sexually." A more intense involvement accompanies that statement.

Many adolescents (one could even say most) have known through toothaches what a paroxysmal pain can be. Rarely do we experience such intense, lasting, and mind-blowing impacts. (Stomach pains, seasickness, hurts, and wounds can also affect us and teach us the "negative" side of feelings.) Rarely do we pursue pain. Generally we shrink from it. But suddenly sexuality offers a field for the exploration of intense feelings and most people plunge into it.

In any case, we all live 24 hours a day with ourselves and always have a few hours to ourselves in which we can entertain a dialogue with one or another of our functionings. Hence, when we discover that our hand can transmit feelings to the self and can relate to a part of ourself in which the self is interested and can dwell, the same self can order the hand to generate more, a flow of feelings of the sources newly discovered. Whether one learns to do this from others, or initiates oneself, is immaterial in this particular examination. We leave it to be what it has been in each particular case. In fact, after that initiation, each person individually will decide what to do, when and how often.

Friction alone can take someone only so far. There must be an evolution of the person on the somatic level to enable him to break through a threshold, which in the male translates itself into ejaculation. No amount of massaging a penis can produce the flow of semen until the total evolution of that male adolescent translates itself into the capacity of the testicles to produce their secretions. But once this capacity is reached, friction leads to orgasm, and this is experienced as an acute pleasure, comparable only to toothache in both intensity and the involvement of the self in the sensation.

It is at this stage that lust can rear its head.

As soon as the self decides that it is important to investigate the new capacity, the psyche can find its place and intervene with the arsenal of powers available for its use. It is the longing for a return to intense pleasure that encourages the person to seek out the occasions in which it can be encountered.

Lust is a state of mind in which greed may insert its proven mechanism, although greed is not a necessary companion.

When we know that lust is a late comer among the functionings of the psyche and that it begins with a legitimate place in the spectrum of behaviors available to the self, we are prepared to look at it for what it is and not as the stigma of a fallen creature.

The many forms taken by lust result only from the fact that the psyche has intelligence, imagination, appetite, and the capacity to forget or ignore as well as the capacity to stress and remember. Lust as such is the return within the self of the move to abandon what one is doing in order to engage in the pursuit of activities that will procure the intense experience of orgasm.

When one yields to its solicitation, one finds in the actuality of life whether it is better for one to go on or to abandon falling for it. Lust can chase all other occupiers of consciousness and incite one to give into its pursuit. If pursued by masturbation alone, lust can gain a taste that the self interprets as a warning that the action has become a non-biological functioning. The bitter taste spurs the self to do something to stop it, to direct the psyche to stop nourishing the self with images and promises that lure one to seek to do it again. If lust is pursued with others, in couples or otherwise, the closure on oneself can be broken, and lust is added to the social indulgences of society.

The working of lust resembles that of greed, except that for males the loss of energy compacted in the semen can trigger a behavior of recuperation through sleep instead of an immediate involvement to repeat. For some males, the capacity to indulge in repeat acts of lust may be very limited, while for others repetition may be easy up to a certain number of times.

Lust as a psychic movement fools the self into believing that the pursuit of pleasure is always a justified human endeavor. Lust affects the subject so as not to demand that the other person be anyone special. Lust can do away with love and can lead to intercourse not only with anyone ready or not ready to copulate but also with animals or mechanical substitutes. The pursuit of pleasure justifies the move in rape, in sodomy, and in all the forms sung in pornographic literature.

Once we have associated lust and selfish behaviors, we have opened the door to moralistic judgments. Lust becomes a behavior to condemn and to get rid of. Penance may be a way of stirring the self to do something about it. Society throws its opprobrium on it, and pressures are exercised by some people upon others to change a condemnation into a punishment. Fears are generated by forcing the imagination to associate lust with punishments all out of proportion to the act itself, like finding oneself in Hell for such pursuits of happiness. One then is distracted by fears and abandons knowing oneself in lust, and instead gives one's energy to guilt and self-deprecation.

On the other hand, not only is lust permissible in some circumstances, such as the nuptial bed; it is sometimes encouraged, if it produces effects desired by those who supervise society. Lust in small amounts is no sin!

In small or large doses, lust is the same functioning, and to free oneself from its impact requires that we understand how it functions in the behaviors sponsored by the self and nourished by the psyche.

Clearly, we are not advocating the elimination of lust as moralists do; we are only advocating that it be understood, leaving to everyone the choice of handling it in his own case, in his unique way.

The human condition can accommodate itself to many absences or presences. A person is not less of a person because lust is or is not at work in him or her. There is not much more merit in being free from lust than being not free of it. Baudelaire's poetry gained much from his acceptance of his lust. Many influential writers have gained fame and influence because they found how to handle the aesthetic part contained in lust for many people.

The watchful person may recognize how the attributes of a person he is looking at can become a source for his lust to be moved. We all know that anatomically a man or a woman is like this or like that. But this knowledge is so superficial that the sight of sane part of the anatomy of the other sex may generate an upheaval. Some words may have become so loaded that their utterance can produce shifts of energy within that make such words dangerous in some circumstances. Lust as a psychic movement seems to be always ready to go to work—much faster than one's logic, one's common sense, or even one's imagination, although the last is so intermingled with lust.

Lust in cooperation with imagination provides a world of human expression exploited by artists everywhere. The stone friezes of Khajuraho in India, The Decameron of Boccaccio, the works of Rabelais, Balzac, and Zola, of Thomas Hardy, and many others, all have exalted the existence of lust as a source of drama and human suspense.

It seems that man is ambivalent about lust. As the source of pleasure at its peak, it is sought by everyone. Still, when given to it, bitterness, guilt, a sense of diminution of one's stature often follows. Lust is known to be connected with love and at the same time separated from it. Lust will make everyone feel in love with lots and lots of people because of the component of infatuation found both in love and in the working of lust, but no one is prepared to love everybody physically. Love is presumed to be for the elected ones. Lust is suspected by the self that experiences it because it seems to be a trap to the spiritual self in every one of us.

So in spite of all, we would all like to be freer from lust so that we can live instead of being lived by it. Is there a way to accomplish this?

Do we attempt to bring to the preadolescent, almost pubescent youth what he or she needs in order for lust to be kept within consciousness, or do we rather wait to meet lust in the post adolescent?

Since lust is a constructed dynamism in the self and is not needed for reproduction (as we see in plants and animals) and results from specific dwellings of the self in some of its objectivations, it is possible to entertain an education of one's consciousness so that the self directly considers sexual pleasure.

Sexual pleasure is attractive because it is so intense and can be obtained so easily by masturbation. Though masturbation teaches that the act by itself is really sterile and is accompanied by a feeling of bitterness, it is not necessary to leave the job of remedying this to the displacement of one's consciousness. The remedy lies in an awareness of the dynamics that transfer the contact with sexuality from the self to the psyche.

If love were not available to mankind, lust would be needed to generate offspring (now that we know that man does not entertain instincts). Lust can be absorbed by love and lovemaking—which need not be at all the expression of lust as it is when male or female prostitutes are made to substitute for one's beloved.

Lovemaking in love is the form given by man to assert his integrity, when the self is given its position at the top and the psyche is given its role as a supplier to the soma and its functionings.

Lovemaking does not require lust. It seems not to need lust when love is present and the self is given through affectivity to meeting the moment. Lust is needed for mere copulation, for the exploration of sex and the adventures dictated by the imagination mobilizing the psychic energy that feeds lust. Sexual relations between unknown people can be an expression of the power of the psyche to mobilize all that love mobilizes. The self feels differently in the two cases—and that makes the differences.

Men and women, because they have access to the energy of their psyche, can use lust to enter into physical relations of all kinds. But because they also know love, they can keep out of such relationships; they can tell themselves that there will be lovemaking only with the loved ones. Then the pull to be with one's beloved is not inwardly acknowledged as lust, in spite of all the appearances.

Then the self commands and is obeyed with one's perception that one's integrity is present and respected, and no other slant is authorized to make its appearances in one's awareness.

Lust can therefore only be checked by love, which like a twin resembles it from outside but inwardly is the other.

To be freer from lust, if one so desires, one can ask how love can reach one and how one can give oneself to love. When this is known, it is possible to discover that although the psyche exists and is functional, although one is capable of lust, lust does not present itself. To be in love is no one's privilege, we are all longing for another that will fulfill us. Giving oneself is the road to love, giving oneself to love, that is. When this is genuine, one can know that lust is no longer the puller of strings that takes away our freedom. And one can know freedom from lust in love.

4 From Ambition

It has been said that if someone has ambition he can get anywhere.

Ambition is the spring motivating everyone to succeed socially.

It is also much more complicated than this, and we must take a look at ambition and its working before we declare it to be of benefit to the individual and, through him, to society.

Ambition is an ego movement and as such belongs to the psyche. This fact makes it neither bad nor good—it just places it—and tells us at once (1) that ambition has the characteristic approaching that of an automatism and (2) that ambition may escape the control of the self and force the self to give up some of its prerogatives.

One can be consumed with ambition and not know it.

One can subordinate all considerations to the realization of one's ambitions.

Examples around us or even in our own lives may at once rush in to illustrate both statements.

The components of ambition are complex. One component involves the intellect, for one must be able to envision a somewhat structured future before taking a course of action directed towards achieving one's goals. Another component involves a direct contact with one's sources of energy, to mobilize them to get what one wants and to arrive where one wants to arrive. Another component is the ability to enter into the intricacies of the social world to discover what ropes one has to pull to accomplish one's ends. Yet another component is the capacity to recast one's experiences in terms of one's project.

As we shall see, there are other components, but these are sufficient to direct our study for now.

The components noted so far all suggest that an ambitious person is a gifted person—that in order to achieve one's ends, one must be attentive to many things—showing perhaps that being ambitious is synonymous with being intelligent, diligent, studious, industrious, etc., all qualities admired in our societies. Hence, everyone may want to encourage ambition in those around them, for their own good and the good of their kin.

It is in fact encouraged, and in the familiar aphorism "Heaven helps those who help themselves," we can read a general encouragement from above.

Still, when we think of man as needing to be freer than he is at this moment, it is clear that ambition is one of the movements that tie him.

Indeed, we all know people who magnify for us the workings of ambition and from whom we get the hint that we should be on our guard not to do as they do.

Most people believe the general statements that man wants to, indeed must, improve himself, and that man seeks greater happiness and finds it by taking himself to certain places and levels, and these statements suggest some of the problems surrounding ambition.

If "to improve myself" is limited to doing all I can for myself and at any cost, many of us would prefer not to encourage improvement. The social approval of ambition as a method of improving oneself generates the danger that those who are insufficiently sensitive or intelligent to look at what they are doing will believe that the ends justify the means.

To study ambition at work we must look at it in those who take it to extremes as well as in those who only toy with it. We must look at its variety and its onset, its installation in the mind of a person, its possession of other functions in order to marshal them towards the objective, its adequacy for achieving the goal, and we must look at how to keep on top of it and subjugate it when it becomes a dysfunction.

When a box is given to a baby, he sometimes attempts to open it. The movement of the mind that gets hold of the given (the box) to make it yield what it might contain can be construed as a sketch of ambition at work; it becomes more so when the baby focuses only on the effort of opening it, forgetting other attractions.

When a girl who has been learning to skip rope tells herself, "I must do it a hundred times in a row," and dedicates herself for days and days to achieving this arbitrary end, ambition is at work. The projection of a goal and working towards it are part of ambition; dedication to its success is also part of ambition.

When a student enters a specialized school to equip himself to compete with others for, say, a special place in a profession, he may have in his mind the resolution that he must gather all he has in order to gain as much as he can from the opportunity offered him at the school and through its contacts. This state of mind is also part of ambition. The effort may add components of steadfastness, stamina, and self-knowledge, which must stand years of exertion.

When a man enters politics in a society where one has to appeal to numerous tastes, reaching the chosen goal requires that the uniqueness of the individual be given up, at least for a while, and that one stress the features and opinions that appeal to and meet widespread prejudices. In these circumstances, ambition is given the right to control all the values and possibilities offered by one's gifts and opportunities. Only what is compatible with the one goal can be pursued and entertained, the reward coming from the feeling of power once one is installed rather than being in the fulfillment of one's gifts.

In the dialogues of the self with itself or aspects of itself, either the central function commands the actualizing of what one finds to be the expression of one's integrity and one's destiny, or the manifestations of oneself in life feedback what one needs to consider further. In the first movement, the self knows every aspect of what occupies its exchange of time into experience. In the second, the self is left open to all sorts of interventions that press for recognition, significance, and importance. The self will be involved in every movement of a person, but that involvement may express the central function as it leads to health or express a response to random impacts, which denies the role of leader to the self.

In the second circumstance, the psyche can respond to demands that prompt one to ignore an obvious truth in order to reach one's goal: one has to stress what may not be relevant in the large to be successful locally; one has to be open to changing one's mind for convenience's sake. All this gives the person the status of one who has lost his freedom, hence is less himself or herself.

Confronted with the dual movement of succeeding socially and failing spiritually, the ambitious individual chooses to be successful, but this makes him unsuccessful at the same time—

unless it were possible to be both socially and spiritually successful, as so many have tried and so very few have managed to be. Ambition may aim at power, and it is known that power corrupts. Ambition may aim at wealth, and often money corrupts.

The psychic movements comprising ambition can be compounded by those of greed. It is symptomatic that the ambitious person is not satisfied when the goal is reached. At once another target appears, and the race is once more on its way. It is therefore not ambition that needs to be checked but the movements of ambition in the ambitious one.

That everyone seeks a position from which he can give back to the world the gifts he has received seems to accord with an enlightened view of social action and social good. That someone in an organization objectively judges that certain functions would be more adequately performed if he occupied a position of command and then does what is necessary to secure such position, may be socially justified. But to catch oneself constantly engaged in attempting to secure higher and higher positions demonstrates that the movement is no longer connected to the original purpose and is now only egocentric.

In addition to the individual aspect of ambition, which shows a person losing control of his destiny and being lived by ambition, there is a social consequence that results from an individual's striving. Competition installs itself in the group, and the law of the fish prevails: the big ones swallow the little ones; the smartest outsmarts the others.

In some societies this is not only acceptable but encouraged, and morality gains an elasticity in the working world that is unacceptable in other areas of living. When this occurs the younger generation may be excused if it is unable to determine what the rules of behavior are in that society. On the one hand, cutthroat action is permitted; on the other, everyone is invited to be decent and helpful to others. This confusion generates in society a malady ever more difficult to pinpoint and cure.

When the psyche commands, it does so as a usurper, and loyalty and allegiance to anything other than the ego are hard to determine. In the environment of unconstrained competition, it is difficult to allow truth as a criterion. Deception is in order as long as one is not exposed.

Ambition may have consequences that are not seen as belonging to it, and the impetus to be free of ambition may be dictated not so much by the fact that individuals are being lived, as by the effects caused by its unchecked presence in society.

To motivate the ambitious to expend their mental energy in the effort to hold in check their tendencies rather than the pursuit of their ends, has always been difficult because the spiritual component, which is involved in such an effort, is not an aspect of social dynamics. Only the self is capable of enlightening the whole mind and of mobilizing the will to produce changes in behavior and the degrees of engagement and involvement. It is therefore necessary to transcend the social level to free oneself from ambition in regard to institutions and status.

If one's ambition is related to universes other than the social one—the intellectual or the magical, for example—then it will be necessary to transcend other functionings too.

Giovanni Papini, the Italian writer, tells the story of his ambition to produce a dictionary in his late teens or early twenties. Although he was truly in contact with his intellectual gifts and was entitled to believe that the task was commensurate with them, he was not in contact with his inner resources and had to give up after composing the entries up to Ab.

In contrast, the Tibetan poet Milarepa, gifted in the ability to summon natural powers and to use them at his discretion, recognized that these powers were of no avail if one wanted to go through one's evolution in one lifetime, and he dropped the use of them.

As part of the effort of the self to project and to move towards goals, ambition may have its place as a function. The thing to look at is the nature of the end. It is the end that determines whether using ambition as a personal trait and giving oneself to it is human or not.

Thus, it appears that a form of ambition can be under the command of the self.

But if ambition is only a movement of the psyche, to indulge in it necessarily means that the pattern of greed will be its form. The individual will find himself on an incline, unable to control the sequence of events.

At the start of this chapter we dogmatically defined ambition as a movement of the ego, hence of the psyche. Now we are questioning this definition, at least hypothetically. To reach a decision may require a better understanding of all the terms.

The self includes the psyche but differs from it because the self has free energy.

The psyche includes the ego but differs from it because not all psychical movements display adherence, the characteristic of the ego.

Clearly, the ambitious individual must adhere to his projection if his movement is to be counted an ambition, even if everything is subconscious.

If in the here and now the self is totally conscious that it is using its energy to forward the accomplishment of the projection, then there is need neither for adherences nor for linking the projection to anything else. Once one realizes the acts performed in the here and now and the projection, the self passes to something else.

But no one recognizes in this description the etiology of ambition. The principal characteristic of ambition is the lingering of the past in the projection. This creates a continuity in the relation of the individual to his acts and makes him note his history and the history of his acts.

This alone forces us to make ambition a psychic creature. But it is more precisely a creature of the ego since adherence is visible at every moment of one's life associated with the objectivation of the actions relevant to the project.

To be free from ambition, the particular adherences must be found, located exactly, and then removed via the surgery of the self, which uses as a scalpel its capacity to withdraw energy from nonsomatic objectivations.

Once the adherences are no longer operative, the self has to examine the context that proposes the project and justifies the ambition. To free the subject from that ambition, the self may offer itself a period of time for activities as valid to the self as were the previous ones to the psyche. In fact, it means engaging oneself in non-egocentric activities compatible with one's gifts and realizable through them.

Whether such activities exist in all cases remains to be proved. Freud believed that sublimation had the power to propose to the patient alternative involvements, and he encouraged them.

What we can keep sight of here is that we need to be freer and freer of ambition simply because it pulls strings that make us be lived rather than live.

5 From Resistances

Stubbornness is not the only form of resistance. Shyness can also be resistance if the will uses it to brake the moves required by the situation.

In professional circles when a new idea is proposed, minds may close up and even oppose the reception of the idea. Often a conspiracy of silence is a most effective resistance to what some individuals do not want to acknowledge or let others acknowledge.

More subtle resistances are to be met in various walks of life.

Interference by one's fears when learning to swim or dive or ski are forms of resistance that teachers know well.

Refusal to enter a game whose effect may be vital for some activity is an open resistance covering a mental resistance.

A common observation about very young children is that they learn to say "no" very early and use the word very effectively. I know a child who said her first "yes" two years after having said "no." This negation is needed to protect the baby from some sorts of coercion from the environment, and it is used, discriminately at first, systematically afterwards, if need be. Then the baby learns how to widen resistance from the physical to the social. Conscious at first, such resistances get buried in one's subconscious and become automatic, creating the many problems psychopathologists often mention.

These studies clearly reveal that resistance is a psychic phenomenon and needs to be known thoroughly before one can attempt to free oneself from it, as indeed many psychotherapies suggest.

But to know resistance at work may require that we separate it from pathology and consider it in its wider frame of operation, the inner life of each of us.

Essentially, the universe can be subdivided into two unequal but equally important segments: the self's part and the rest. While the rest is much larger and more varied than the first, it is in the first that we have access to the dynamics that permit the second to exist for each one of us.

We are not only egocentrically the most important person on Earth, we are, to ourselves, the only truly knowable speck of the universe. Knowledge stems from within, and man makes sense of his impressions—not the other way around.

Constantly bombarded by what the non-self sends out, we cannot fail to notice that we are endowed with a stressing and ignoring apparatus that cuts into the totality to let some things in and to keep most things out. Thanks to this apparatus we can chart our own way in the wilderness and produce the unique life that is ours, distinct even from the lives of those immersed in the same environment as ourselves.

From such a system, which protects our life in the chaos, we draw the means to make sense of what we individually let in.

Now imagine two such systems (that is, two people) in relationship with each other and imagine that one system stresses something different from what the other stresses but also attempts to interest the other in it. The "natural" origin of resistance is at once made plain. Resistance "to being with" is the expression of the individual's rights to be engaged in what matters to him rather than what matters to others.

From this we can see how in the complex of relationships each of us will encounter in ourselves any number of resistances every day. Most times we do not mind, first, because we are realists and at least sometimes take things as they are and, second, because we fall so easily into our own preoccupation or occupations that we ignore the others.

But sometimes we do mind, and it is then that we meet resistance.

In our inner dialogue we may quickly brush away the resistance, assigning it to some psychic suggestion, and maintain a status quo. Or we may wonder why we are resisting and learn something about ourselves. We may also use the resistance to study resistance, how it is generated, entertained, and handled by one's self.

In the first case we use the well-established procedure of ignoring.

In the second case the dialogue does not require that we remove the resistance, only that we have a basis for its presence and so find a justification for it. For instance, a child may be asked something by a grownup, who only hears the words he or she utters, but the child may also perceive in the tone some patronizing streak and therefore respond negatively to the seemingly innocuous words, producing for the adults a confusion about why the child did not give a straight answer and resisted all invitations "to be polite." A child invited to share in the eating of an apple, say, and who had agreed to do so a number of times, suddenly responds with "No thank you," creating in the offerer thoughts unrelated to the situation. "Did I offend him or her?" the adult may think, instead of asking, "Is it possible that this child sees that getting into a pattern and a routine means a loss of choice and freedom and that the refusal provides a warning that we better stop offering automatically?"

In the last example, the grownups also learn some lessons, even if the mechanism of setting a resistance is not examined. Life is full of examples in which lessons can be learned about why resistances are created and how they can be avoided.

Resisting requires the use of the will. But in stubbornness, for example, the psyche uses the will for its own purposes.

One can resist being touched by others by inviting all sorts of distractions. Thoughts, images, discourses can all supply material for the self to busy itself with rather than give itself to relating, to listening, to participating. This kind of resistance is called on by all those who do not think it profitable to do what is asked of them—for example, school children in many traditional classes where teachers request students to do what is of no interest to them, or children at home who prefer to go on with what they are doing rather than obey their parents. In some relationships, one of the partners may be wholly predictable, and it might be beneficial for the other partner to resist being involved in some connections and to call in distractions that may have greater value in the exchange of one's time for experience.

One strange resistance is resistance to what may be much more in our best interest than the activity we engage in spontaneously. A priori one would think that since we are all moved mainly by self-interest, when we find something that may serve us better, we would at once cooperate wholeheartedly with what has come our way. Instead, we prefer mainly to go on with our routine.

It may be that we do not have enough imagination to conceive that we will change quickly enough to minimize losses and increase gains.

It may be that we are stuck to our past and will not let ourselves get a necessary insight. This failure prevents us from mobilizing our will to produce the desired change, the result being that resistance prevents the self from having a chance.

On the other hand, it may be that one can see beyond what is offered and genuinely know one's best interest because common sense is at work, and one may resist producing a change even though the request is accompanied by the assertion that it is in one's best interest. Such situations particularly involve areas of uncertainty, like sterilization of fathers or birth control or integration of groups. When common sense is at work, resistance is generally justified, for it is our common sense that guides us in our meetings with the unknown and that suggests wise steps. So in such cases, rather than becoming freer from resistance, one finds oneself free to resist. The self then is in command, and this guarantees that one acts as freely as is possible.

It may be too that one knows that there are priorities to consider at a particular moment and that one must resist entering into certain activities now, even though one knows that they are worthwhile, and that they are to be taken up later, even though they may become the most important activities in life once they are entered upon. Some people know that such postponement is possible only for non-vital challenges and do not consider the decision a foolish move, only possibly, an unwise one. The urgency felt by one person may not be felt by another. Still, both use their lights honestly, genuinely. Resistance to conversion is difficult for the converted to conceive, but it is obviously possible. Proselytizers, zealots are impatient when confronted with such resistance, but they cannot reduce it to nothing. Knowing themselves to be on the side of "truth" gives them the impression that there should be no resistance to their suggestions.

In fact, truth is only compelling for those vulnerable to it.

Truth can fail to reach people simply because these people do not open up to it. This does not mean that they resist truth. No one can resist truth. But one can be absorbed in other moves and fail to let truth reach one. This may be a subtle form of resistance.

Can one resist resistance? Or does the move toward freedom extract from each resistance the energy placed in it? Both are possible. In the first case, the self invests in some psychic move that associates with each resistance a countermove that does not allow the resistance to be formed. In the second case, the self, working on the energy mobilized for a resistance, stops the process and removes the energy to make it available as free energy for future use. A person watchful of the inner movements of energy may be alerted to this process, and thus may see to it that no resistance is formed in the presence of requests from people or the environment.

But there still remains the job of becoming free of all the subconscious resistances that have been formed. This task may require some help.

6 From One's Cultural Conditionings

Millions of men and women have emigrated from country to country after wars and cataclysms. Since 1945 so many have moved over our planet that we can speak of an actual phenomenon when we consider what people do to come out of one cultural conditioning and try to enter into another.

Their involvement in that change will help us to recognize that it is done, and this may teach all of us how to free ourselves from our cultural conditionings.

It does not occur to people who do not emigrate that they are culturally conditioned. Being culturally conditioned means little to them because the process has been slow and has continued throughout their lives. But when one finds oneself shifting from one environment to another, one feels a considerable shock, and it often leads to decisions that such a shift is difficult and not worth the effort.

To reach a satisfactory understanding of the process and its demands, we have to consider simultaneously those who manage the change and those who do not.

Man is an extremely adaptable creature. He is found at all latitudes, longitudes, altitudes, in all climates, reliefs, conditions of humidity and heat. Men demonstrate this adaptability in planes, submarines, and boats; in groups or isolation; in jails and concentration camps; eating the best and the worst; going through all sorts of demands put upon their bodies, their minds, and their consciences.

There are many bilingual people, some trilingual, and a few multi-lingual, proving that the same soma can be used for a number of different functionings.

A young person can acquire any of the six thousand or so languages in the world, one as easily as another. When trained in a circus, he can use his body in ways that defeat the imagination of the public. And every year, there are more and more of these incredible uses of a body that seems to be like all other bodies.

If man is so adaptable, why does he not continue to adapt? Why do we become held by cultural conditioning?

There is something in growing up that takes away powers that function in childhood. There is in each of us at a certain stage evidence of powers that could be tapped more fully, perhaps as well as some of us manage to tap some of our powers.

In our not-so-conscious evolution, we may do things to ourselves that infiltrate those parts of ourselves and thus make us appear to be stiff, functioning below the potential we showed in early childhood.

It is one of the purposes of this study to identify some of these things so as to free those who want to be freer from the process of reducing our possibilities.

Let us first note that objectivations are not all somatic. The self, well acquainted with structuring and functioning at the somatic level, has applied such an approach a number of times on the level that flows in time. That is, we can find again and again that the self offers itself structures, organizations, institutions, that lock up energy as hardware, while in and on them, functionaries, like software, use them for the purposes of the self. Thus, language is an institution partly somatic and partly functional, used by the linguistic powers of the self to express the self and through this expression to communicate with others.

We can easily find an analogy in society.

Social agencies are organizations using social structures to perform social ends. Such agencies constitute entities that formerly did not exist, and those who work in them emulate biological functionings. Energy (material and funds) is locked up in these objectivations, and only the residual energy, that of the activities of the workers, can be used to run the functions of the institutions.

It is easy to see structure in the soma or in social institutions; it is harder to see functions in both, although epistemologically, only the function justifies the structure. It is harder still to see structures in some functionings: for example, structures in a language, structures in mathematics, structures in the mind. (These structures are accessible only if one gives oneself special lightings, some of which are found in my earlier works, in particular The Universe of Babies and The Mind Teaches the Brain.)

Let us stay with the example of language.

In a given environment we very early give ourselves a language, that of the environment. We pick it up from the users as one of their functionings, but we also construct it from scratch, using the functionings of our soma and brain.

We objectify all the automatisms needed to generate the noises that belong to the physical universe. These noises are not structures. They are arbitrary signs used for definite grammatical functions, and are adaptable to the rendering of perceptions, actions, feelings, thoughts. Soon the consistencies in the uses of the noises generate a mental structure as complex as the previous mental structures and as usable for carrying on life functions. A language is as recognizable by its structures and features as is any soma.

The new structure of language, although functionally resting on top of the somatic structure (the vocal cords, for example) is experienced as independent and is used as an automatism of the self. There is no need to think of the vocal cords and the rest of the voice production system when speaking or singing. The energy of the self is instead given to one's thought or intention, and this mental process uses the psyche to mobilize the soma for the utterances.

Now, when confronted with a new set of uses of the soma, a new language, for example, the self may panic because the psyche has made the soma available for so long that the self is accustomed only to engaging in the energy that uses the functionings. Suddenly it is asked to descend into the somatic functionings at one or two stages removed from where it usually is at work. The task is even newer now than it was during infancy, for at that time the self was so close to its somatic structure that there was no need to break through anything. Now the culture barrier, although purely mental, is experienced as an impregnable fortress. One is so accustomed to having one's thoughts being immediately transmuted into utterances, highly structured and highly tested for efficiency, that to find them existing as thoughts away from the soma and with no receptacle to descend upon, may truly generate a feeling of falling into a vast void and an ensuing feeling of anxiety.

Languages can cause the greatest demand on new immigrants particularly if they (1) are of a certain age, (2) have been monolingual most of their life, and (3) have been exposed to ways of learning that do not respect their needs (as analyzed above).

But languages are only one of the cultural conditionings suffered by all people on Earth.

There are sets of habits that have long been unconscious and that suddenly break through and call for attention.

Pride in punctuality or neglect of punctuality are displayed in certain cultures, and new demands either to observe or not to observe it are each as painful as the other.

A reversal of attitudes toward work—from regarding it as the most important adult function to tolerating it only in order to have enough money, or vice versa—can put one at odds with a new environment.

A particular attitude to people of the opposite sex, which either ignores them socially or worships them or considers them as equal, is equally difficult to replace genuinely, even though one can pay lip service to the change.

Attention to amenities, or indifference to them, are as much distinctive impacts from one's culture as is language, and is more immediately difficult to change.

The list is much longer, and its particulars hamper not only immigrants. Tourists can be dumb struck by the customs of neighbors, of so-called civilized nations that they visit, and the neighbors can be equally shocked when they return the visit. It is not always true that the neighbor's grass looks greener; sometimes it looks less attractive.

The attachment to the country of one's birth, the acceptance of its way of life, the identification with some of its answers to universal challenges concerning expression, communication, feeding, evacuation, rituals, morals, etc., are so widespread that they must have a profound source in each of us. Some call it fear of the unknown; others, detestation of change.

It may be neither. It may be a more complex response.

How can one feel free when one has to devote one's time to acquiring what one does not have? The investment in habits is not merely for conformity. Conformity is an appearance and the consequence of having acquired some habits. We give ourselves habits because we know that the automatisms we create permit our self to cope with the new, make it free for that.

When our habits become inoperative, it is as though the self must go back and start afresh, revealing the past to be a dead loss as far as today is concerned. If the new habits we need to form are costly in time and effort, we may resent still more giving up our benefits for what may not be successful, as is the case when learning a new language. The self, startled by its incapacity to assess the real cost of moving out of one set of conditionings and acquiring another, may forego its main function, which is to meet the unexpected, the new, and it may join the psyche in nourishing the past in oneself. Reminiscing, it may repeat Dante's line: "Nessun maggior dolor . . .".

This, of course, does not apply to the young or to the more adventurous adults. The first has not yet invested enough in the past to let the psyche subjugate the self. The new environment is after all an environment, and one adapts to it, takes it in one's stride.

As to adventurous adults, they can be of several kinds. Ambitious adults will consider that a certain price must be paid to restore oneself to the place one held in the previous culture. Both the psyche and the self are mobilized, the first using the second to overcome obstacles and to take on all the forms, if not the spirit, of the culture one is in. Some of these adults even become more monarchist than the king, more identified with some expressions of that culture than the natives. But they know deep down that they belong to another culture, which is nourished by nostalgia and is better known and assimilated than this one will ever be. For these adults, if only nothing had happened . . .

Resigned adults proceed more slowly. They seek the company of their kin, and they undertake, little by little and as carefully as possible, the moves that will permit them to have contacts with their hosts, the majority. Their longing for the past is tempered by the presence of people who are at various stages on the road to assimilation. What little desire they have for assimilation is motivated only by their recognition that here is the land of their immediate and perhaps permanent future. They may go to school to acquire the new language, they may accept jobs away from their immediate community, they may adopt some of the outward signs of the hosts, but they are not yet able to see themselves in a wider habitat in a way that requires them to be in it naturally. For their sight is on the appearances, on the obstacles.

Other adults have kept in themselves enough of the adolescent to consider their new country as an opportunity to know themselves as having the gifts of adaptation. They can find in themselves the powers that made them grow in their original environment and can feel these powers to be available for moving first spiritually and physically in the part of the cosmos they occupy (their true habitat) and then socially in their new historical gathering, which did not come into being all at once any more than did the culture they left behind. The order of the encounter in such adults is important, as it is the opposite of what the ambitious person wants to do and the timid one will not attempt.

To know oneself as being born somewhere only because of the physical limitations of size and place, not because of any fate that sent us to a specific spot for specific purposes, already prepares one for coming out of the circumstances of one's birth and meeting the circumstances of other human beings. The spiritual move about our habitat presents us with the truth that we are first human—Earthian—and only secondarily this or that. The physical move at once proves that we can walk on the new land just as we walked on other lands, can breathe the air of both, can drink the water of both. Socially, we can be set apart, or even discriminated against, barred from the opportunities offered others simply because we are not yet part of the groups around us, because open houses are generally rare or reserved for kinsfolk, which by definition we are not.

If we place social integration last, we can find our place in the new culture, and no one will press for a faster assimilation than can actually take place in our circumstances. In fact, we shall be left alone, if only because people are busy with their own affairs and have not much desire to add to their burdens by taking on ours.

Only recently—a little more than a century ago—has man come to the awareness that he is a social being, and this awareness has blurred the awareness of other properties. He still has to become aware of the primitiveness of his cosmic nature, or even his Earthian nature. Instead, he sticks to his culture, to physical conditions as if they were natural, and he tells himself that he cannot come out of his cultural conditionings—any more than he can come out of his soma—without dying, although this is disproved every day. The social conditionings have taken root deep in the psyche, and since the psyche is in contact with the soma, one can easily mistake a psychic condition for a somatic one—a fact known to psychiatrists. But there are profound differences between these conditions, as the self and the will can show. Enlightened by reflection from within or by inspiration from without, the self can see that the soma is being used by cultural behaviors while the soma displays human behaviors. The latter include the brain, while the former are constructs, objectified mental structures far more labile than the somatic structures, and therefore far more easily undone and dissolved.

Images can be de-energized, memories can be de-energized and languages buried in the psyche, thus enabling one to seek new involvements and to find one's place in the new milieu, as long as those in control of the environment make no extravagant demands.

All this is concerned only with the movements of the self away from existing forms in the psyche. It does not imply that hosts are angels, that no exploitation is possible, that no injustice exists. In a later chapter on duties, we touch on rights; here, it is not our purpose to do so.

The fact that people can come out of their past cultural ties proves that these ties are not strong enough to be considered as locked-up energy. A correct description of our cultural conditionings is that they are made of partially structured residual energy and therefore can be reduced in their impact, importance, and momentum by the direct intervention of the self. We sometimes see conditionings, and conclude that they are as indelible as somatic conditionings. But in fact, what has happened is that the self has been defeated by the psyche and has given in to the past.

If such people could only be persuaded that the tasks they believe to be so enormous are not really beyond them, then their self could use its will to alter behaviors and thus render each of them human again—free to use the new.

Hitler had to tell his people to think of themselves as Germans first and as humans second, for such a perspective was not the obvious thing for them. Those who can forget their humanity forget their original condition and adhere to a local one. But Hitler's "truth" failed to reach everyone, and its fallacy is now obvious; people who dwell in their psyche can go one stage deeper and find the human condition in the soma and its functionings and in the capacity to create cultures compatible with them.

To free themselves from cultural conditionings has been almost a necessity for the displaced persons in human history. Is it less so for those who remain in one place?

Today, when our Earthian nature is acknowledged as a fact, when most of our activities are becoming more global and more universal, the pressure from outside on all inhabitants of Earth is to move away from identifying with any one culture. To be free from such ties one needs to discover the phenomenon of adherence and to work on it in order to reduce its dominion over us.

Adherence, as we noted in the introduction, is a psychic move, mobilizing more energy than one requires to be in contact with a certain functioning, thereby making the adhered-to-element more important in one's psychic life than it otherwise would be. It is the definition of the self that it can withdraw energy from adherences.

Intellectually we must understand two things: (1) that we may adhere just because we have had no reason to observe the pouring of energy into any one of the functionings we engage in; and (2) that once we have been placed face to face with an adherence, the undoing of it is another activity for which we may not have prepared ourselves.

Consequently, not everyone is motivated to dissolve adherences, and even those who are, may not always be able to manage it.

Watchfulness can help in not producing new adherences, but it cannot do much to dissolve old ones.

The price one must pay in accomplishing this can be reduced if one works on the least loaded of the adherences first, for instance, acquiring a new language. In the process of succeeding, one can find that if one can mobilize oneself to that extent in such a vast and complex area, then one might also succeed in other areas where emotions are still actively defending the past.

If groups of people of good will were interested in providing such a re-education as a tool for human expansion, whereby people learn to include themselves in a new culture as one more form of being on Earth rather than as the condition for survival, it is today possible to work out in positive terms the procedure that will free people from adherences and enable them to use the recuperated energy to find their increased powers. As a result, the tasks will be less susceptible to failure, and the subjects will do their job as conscious beings who use their will for what it can do: change behaviors.

7 From One's Gifts

For years I recognized dimly that gifts could be handicaps towards being more oneself and freer to enter the true challenges of human life. I let examples strike me and accumulated some, for I wanted to be clear on this matter. In the beginning I did not quite know my gifts. Slowly, as I managed to recognize them, I more and more found that I had to watch their working and, in particular, the way they imposed themselves, naturally.

One of my gifts was a very good memory.

It served me well and quickly helped me gain a sufficient acquaintance with fields of scholarship to elicit the admiration of people younger than myself and the respect of my peers and my elders. I gave myself tasks which bordered on the ridiculous, such as knowing the numerous bus routes of the London Transport and the fares for many trips within the system. Since it was easy for me, I managed it readily. But what alerted me to the dangers of such a gift was the fact that I often would catch myself going over the routes from #1 to #725, telling myself what I knew about the routes, and which ones were not represented by buses now on the roads, etc.

I similarly considered it worth my while to put down on paper as many geographical names as possible starting with successive letters of the alphabet in, say, 3 or 5 minutes. Had I not gained an interest in watching how my memory worked from day to day, this exercise would certainly have meant very little in terms of giving my life a meaning and would have taken away some precious time from other studies.

Another of my gifts, one I did not recognize immediately, was my ability to pass from words to images and actions and, conversely, to verbalize my vision. It served me well in my self-taught studies of chemistry and physics when I was unable to find laboratories to work in (and to adapt to equipment in laboratories when I did). But it was a bad handicap as a teacher, for I automatically imagined that my students had the same gift, and I led many of them to complete confusion as I bombarded them with words that did not trigger in them the same images.

True, when I became aware of that gift, I started studying its functioning and gave attention to how I could fortify its functioning in others. But it was clearly a gift that served as an obstacle to understanding the ways of learning that were open to those without it or who had a less developed ability, and it was a handicap in my study of writers who did not require it. For instance, the approach of all the moralists and philosophers who use language to evoke insights into what does not require imagery could easily have escaped me and left me as closed to their message as any illiterate would be.

Another gift in many is imagination.

It is so much fun to let one's imagination run wild or to spend time entertaining it for producing words of art, that one could and often does easily indulge this gift of imagination at the expense of other avenues of life. This is a subtle point, for most of us use as a criterion for a good life the fun we get from living it. Another deceptive use of one's gifts is to contribute to the world's good by doing what is valued by others: works of art and good deeds.

Since we are studying in this book how to become freer from all that may take us away from what could be considered a proper human end for the use of one's time, our answers may well differ from current views. In fact, until one has studied more seriously what is offered to each of us as actual fulfillment of one's self, all proposals may be thought of as clichés and considered a priori as revisable.

Since I am not acting as a moralist, I am not proposing "shoulds," only looking at what gifts do to us. They can be distracting elements in one's life and can make it harder to concentrate on what one could do if one reached the state of being able to see what life truly offers each of us.

Clearly, being endowed with sex organs is a gift. But all religious leaders have known that to indulge in the use of that gift makes one less able to give oneself to other pursuits that are as valuable to the self as procreation (which is vegetable and animal) and pleasure, and are perhaps more human.

Clearly, having the "gift of gab" is no guarantee that one will use the gift to enhance what one would know needed enhancing if one's gifts were used differently. One can use words eloquently for ends not seriously justifiable except on grounds of ego-fulfillment.

Clearly, the immediate exploitation of one's gifts may conflict with one's interests if they were better understood—as so many young people find when, having given themselves one hundred percent to some activity (say, sports), they find themselves totally unprepared to enter life after suffering an accident that precludes the coveted career.

There are two questions here: (1) do people really know what their gifts are, and (2) do they know which gifts should be pursued in order to live one's life as a human being instead of being lived by some move taken with a dim awareness?

There may be gifts to be wary of and others to be aware of. There may be gifts we want to free ourselves from and others we should first find and then inquire whether or not we want to use them for the realization of ourselves in the world.

Because most of us allow ourselves to be shoved along certain paths and, soon after, to be identified with them, there is good reason to ask seriously, "Must I become free of my gifts?"—that is, become freer of them everyday.

The real way of knowing one's gifts involves us in a watchfulness which most of us stopped using quite early in our childhood.

For instance, the gift of suspending judgment has left most of us. We are quick to let mechanisms replace this functioning, which keeps most babies free from accusing others of what they know starts in themselves, free from placing on people coming close to them a ready-made response because of superficial impacts, including skin color, age, and garments. Suspending judgment is a gift, not a built-up behavior and response. In fact, it is not considered by psychology writers as worthy of their attention because only sages make use of it, and there are too few of them around. Still, it is demonstrated by young babies day in and day out, and for a few years, it may still be available to them in spontaneous learning.

Those of us who know this gift and see it as one that serves to correct the function of others, may recognize that, as a gift that frees, it would be absurd to try to be without it. In fact, those who are without it may discover that it can be of great assistance in so many ways of life that it pays to save it from oblivion.

The gift of patience is another valuable state of mind that we bring with us when we are born. It consists in knowing that processes take their time and that to be "with" one of them means to give the time it takes to perform what its inner demands require. In all of our spontaneous learning since conception, we have all demonstrated the gift of patience. But most of us, when we let our ego gain the upper hand in our life, lose this precious ally of our functionings. We become not only impatient—the opposite of patient—but also waste time justifying what we do. We may even consider our impatience as the gift and mistake our wasting time as a capacity for quick, right judgments.

Patience accompanies being "with" a process and is equivalent to recognizing that every process will display its truth and that tampering with the process means a lack of understanding of the phenomenon one is with. Patience is required if one seeks the truth, if one meets the unknown, which is everyone's lot but is still not recognized by everyone.

To become freer every day requires that we return every day to being more patient as a general insight into the fact that we are surrounded by mystery, are very ignorant of vital components in our searches, and need a lot of help almost all the time to lead our bark to safer waters. Patience is not a virtue; it is a necessity in our human condition and in most circumstances. We have it as a gift, built into our somatic and later growth. We can perpetuate it simply by recognizing what it does to us. Education, that is, self-education, can do the job of bringing to our notice the awareness that patience is to be conceived as an ally of conscious living.

Common sense, as its name indicates, is supposed to belong to all of us. Still, the French philosopher Henri Bergson could rightly remark that it is "the least common of all the senses!" As a gift, it means that we are endowed with the power to see things as they are. Why is it, then, that we all seem to lack precisely that very power and look for answers where they are not?

Among the tales of Sufi wisdom is the story of the man who one evening lost a precious coin or stone in the street and started looking for it under a street light. A group of passers-by joined him in his search as soon as they learned he was looking for a precious stone. After a period of unsuccessful efforts, a new person who was going to join in the search asked: "Where did you lose it?" The answer astonished everybody. "Out there," said the man pointing to a spot some distance away. "But why then do you look for it here?" asked all those in the party. "Because there is no light out there, and there is some here."

This story tells us how we manage to cancel our common sense. Instead of being with what we need to be with, we give ourselves to all sorts of other things: we believe what we read; we endow people with qualities and powers they may not have and then we believe that they have them; we deny obvious things and pursue impossible tasks; we value ideals even when they have no chance of being made real; we refuse to look at truth and willingly become gullible when lies are presented to us in an imposing garb; we consider false or non-existent what we do not understand; we confuse age with wisdom and high position with real merit; we are ready to be insolent with someone we do not know, even if that person could have claim to our respect, and show respect to someone soon to be proved unworthy of it; we give ourselves to following what others follow, seeing some value in this, although we may be following a fad sponsored by selfish people for selfish reasons; we mistake the search for truth for many things it is not—personal criticism, personal enhancement, personal interest; we run away from ourselves by remaining what we were in other locations, positions, situations.

Common sense would take care of all this, but we do not permit it to, simply because we have developed adherences to all these dysfunctions and because the ego can fool the self. To give common sense its right to help the self in its complex tasks may be the freeing we need from all these gifts of ourselves represented by these dysfunctions. (Gift has two meanings, either a given, received somehow and brought with us in this life, or the giving of oneself to something, whatever it is.)

To be fair to the task of freeing ourselves, we must include the many jobs of recuperating the functions of common sense from the gift of ourselves to what does not warrant it.

While such freeing may gain acquiescence quite readily, the harder, less acceptable task of freeing oneself from the gifts that flatter the self (or rather the psyche and the ego), is the real challenge.

Yet it is possible to become humble and modest without forcing oneself into the paths of humiliation and self-negation if one finds that indeed there is no merit associated with whatever gifts one can count as one's endowment from birth or from previous lives. This vision of one's gifts (including beauty, energy, sensitivity) as being as much a part of life as one's so-called handicaps, will lead one to see that each life is unique and not in competition spiritually with another, and that the components that make of the uniqueness of our life its most important characteristic, do indeed achieve simply that, thereby giving worth to everybody and hence to us.

We are freer from our gifts when we relate to the whole of our evolution, in this life, in all our lives, with the cosmos as our habitat; freer when we see how often we do not use ourselves as we might; freer when we recognize that although we cooperate with life to take ourselves where we are as successful people, we need a great deal of luck to see so many favorable circumstances come together to our advantage; freer when we enter the complexity of being in a complex inner and outer environment—seeing how often we have missed the possibly costly consequences of a poor functioning of ours and of others around us, and meeting the mystery of our survival amidst ignorance and neglect; freer when we count as gifts the innumerable near-misses or near-hits that pave our daily lives and the happenings whose consequences could have been out of proportion to their causes; freer when we learn to consider each day as another to test our wisdom and our common sense; freer when we manage to reach the springs of life in our inner life and cooperate with them.

It seems that we could be freer by checking the claims of the psyche on what we do with ourselves. But such a dialogue is difficult because our gifts have the nature of natural phenomena and seem inevitable, necessary, dictated by forces beyond us.

To make this checking possible, the self must entertain affectivity, which is not attached to the content of the psyche.

Affectivity, as we saw in the introductory chapter, relates to the unknown, and the demands of that unknown bring about gifts not mortgaged to the past, gifts that do not seem natural but which, when the self recognizes them and passes them on to the psyche, may one day join the list of past gifts.

Affectivity, which does not work through memory, is free and can let the self entertain the new. The gift of surrendering and the gift of respecting are both generated by affectivity as soon as the self agrees to let the unknown find its way in us. Through surrender to what comes our way, we affirm our will not to let the past occupy the new nor the known reduce the unknown. Through respect for what comes, we give ourselves the states to receive it intact.

The gift of oneself to others, when it is non-calculating, not expecting anything in return, non-demanding, is a true gift, free from the outset and kept free by the vigilant self (which is capable of knowing at once that it has shifted position, altered states). Affectivity renews its dwelling in those renewable and renewed relationships, keeping them free of the possession that the psyche commands. The gift of oneself to others that manages to have these dimensions is known as unconditional, though not timebound; as realistic, though unaffected by facts; as profound, though not involving feelings; as created by the others, for each singularly.

The gifts that affectivity awakens and makes known to the self are sometimes also triggered by circumstances not sought out by the person. Job's story tells us of his many gifts before he received the signs that all his friends called calamities. When he found in their presence that he had mortgaged his relationship to God, he looked for the gifts in him that made him acknowledge each calamity as a gift unknown to him and capable of increasing his relationship to God—making it truer, purer, more that of the man of faith he was and wanted to be.

Ramakrishna, when he discovered the cancer of his throat which he kept to his death, did all he could to understand its presence as a mark of the love of Kali; it made him know himself renewed.

The gift of transcending pain, suffering, sorrow, while living them intensely makes the self know itself as free.

Saint Theresa of Avila and Saint John of the Cross knew all that came their way as gifts and received what others would call the blows of adversity as blessings sent by God. They had the gift of total faith which eliminated the working of the psyche, which made them free. Affectivity dwells in faith and gives it its color of optimism in any adverse circumstance.

To be free from one's gifts may require that we learn to accept as gifts what are called handicaps and to recognize that in the actuality of living there are extraneous elements that force us to understand why the so-called handicaps are helping our evolution. The gift of linking previous lives with this life, and of seeing each successive life as part of what one has to do to reach the self in evolution, may carry with it the perception that we no longer speak of handicaps or gifts but of the given, potential as well as actualized, which in the vicissitudes of our lives become known. The given that agrees with one's evolution constitutes one's gifts, that which hampers it constitutes one's handicaps, but both relate to the self and its functionings, giving each of us our entries into the consciousness of what we are.

To become freer of one's gifts is no easier than to become freer of one's handicaps, nor more difficult; it consists in using our watchfulness to the point that we see we are being helped or hampered in what we do with ourselves, within our awareness of our evolution. Then gifts can become handicaps and conversely, and our work on ourselves the gift that frees us from both.

8 From One's Duties

In an orthodox Hindu family, it is considered appropriate for a man who has raised his family, and done what is expected of him by the community, to leave the community and his family and go to the forest to take care of himself as a being evolving beyond the somatic and the social levels. Not all Hindu men choose this path, but if they do, the community does not raise objections; on the contrary, it praises the move as being in conformity with a cosmic sense of life that allows each individual to take himself to any level of consciousness he may attain.

Outside Hinduism any such move is usually considered to be one of escape and evasion, a mark of selfishness, of misunderstanding.

Using the lights of consciousness and common sense, let us examine what lies behind our sense of duty.

In animals we find a spectrum of behaviors expressing a biological and instinctual trend that associates a sense of not neglecting the needs of others to some fixed actions that take care of the needs. From the purely functional relationship of the male praying mantis to the female (to take his fertilizing sperm to the females and then to be discarded—by being devoured!) to the highly organized community of ants or bees, who allow members to live only to continue the sequence of generations, there are all sorts of mixtures of individual independence and autonomy, on the one hand, and bonds that more or less tie for varying durations, on the other.

Over the generations and in a number of separate valleys, people on Earth have examined their position and have called duty what, for the sake of others, they are ready to accept as restrictions on the expression of their individuality. Duties became more organized in some societies than in others, and public opinion as well as laws have regulated the way people are allowed to move the boundaries in either direction.

In the first books of the Pentateuch, two stories tell us that a community with access to consciousness and conscience wanted to give successive generations examples on which to meditate. The Old Testament is full of references to duty, but the story of Onan and that of Tamar are particularly helpful here.

According to tribal custom, Onan was asked to fertilize his brother's widow, and while taking advantage of the law to make love to his sister-in-law, he withdrew his gift of sperm and made it useless on the soil. The reason given was that he objected to his progeny being considered his brother's and not his. Here we need retain only that physical withdrawal in the act of procreation was as powerful as the tribal laws, since it reduced one of them to nothing. All the dialogue in the story is at the level of the mind, all the drama is at the point where individual's rights and the community's demands meet. The story was kept in the Bible for the illumination of succeeding generations, who were supposed to give time to side either with Onan or with the tribal tradition.

The story of Tamar again illustrates how the ordinary people in the Hebrew tribe considered the role of the laws at the individual level. One duty of the head of a family was to make one of his sons, a younger brother, marry the widow of an older brother. Tamar was a widow and her father-in-law was doing nothing on her behalf, so she decided to force him to an awareness of his duty. She went to a market that he was to visit and offered herself to him, veiled as a prostitute. After they had intercourse, she revealed herself and the reason of her move, namely, to remind him of his duties.

Duties involve people, traditions, freedoms, and the surrender of some freedoms so as to contribute to a smooth running of life, which is complex, unpredictable, and invites participation, biologically, sociologically, psychologically.

Biologically, duties are connected with basic needs, as in the case of animals. Those who cannot fend for themselves—and they are still to be found in the world after millennia—must be supported by the activities of others. For this to happen, there must be both a built-in sensitivity to the needs of the dependent and know-hows that will lead adults to take the necessary specific steps. The complexes connected with such moves have been studied by animal observers and are amazing in their precision, variety, and adequacy. If man is considered to be an animal, he may have access to such mechanisms. But if man is taken to belong to a realm beyond animals, as is maintained here, he can look at everything and take steps that demonstrate his individual lights and will, steps that may counter collective moves.

Mankind has organized the environment sociologically and freed some people from some duties, which are taken over by others. Collectively, individuals reach an understanding that it is acceptable to give up some freedoms (to take on some duties) to obtain in return something judged as freedom also (rights). Hence, in the family the social contract means that contributing one's time and some know-hows entitles one to rights acceptable to others, who then find themselves having duties ipso facto.

Both duties and rights are internal movements of the mind, which knows them well enough to distinguish and label them. The dynamics take place within the individual, but because of how the self works, they are projected and objectified in society. So individuals sometimes find themselves at loggerheads with each other and misinterpret reality. In fact, they construct a reality within Reality and identify with the first, consequently truncating the second and even distorting it.

Once we have given our thought of society, community, nation, family, etc., the label of reality, we are enmeshed in a duality that does not offer us two equally reachable components. When we link with ourselves, we do not have the same wealth of content as when we link with the "outside" world. Indeed, while there are a large number of items that can come together as images to form frescoes for our life, the self's work is in time, is axial for our awareness, and produces a climate rather than actual content—like feeling the melody of a long song or of an opera rather than the tale in it. This feeling can summon images and form a display that the reality of our thought cannot. It remains a feel and can be objectified only using as much time as the melody.

When we link with ourselves, duties weigh much more than rights. To stress rights becomes a matter of stressing duties to oneself and of generating rival duties.

Wealth of content brings about guilt in those who neglect duties but not when rights are being neglected. And guilt is a function of the psyche, since guilt concerns the past—when one made promises one did not fulfill or heard stories that put a tone in one's life leading people to expect that one would behave in a prescribed manner. Those who are made to feel guilty when their rights are not taken care of have changed rights into duties.

When we say, "I owe this to so and so or to that thing," we tell ourselves that one aspect of our consciousness has become engaged in evaluating actions and to giving greater value to some actions than to others. Consciousness has become conscience.

Duty is one of the climates of conscience. Conscience not only makes us believe that we are free only when we discharge our duty but that perhaps there is no life worth living other than one in which we do our duty.

When conscience gains such an important status in the self, the freedom of the self expresses itself only through the functionings of the psyche. The person no longer claims to have a self, does not know what freedom could be, does not seek to be more than the realization of the best performer of one's duties.

Orthodoxies of all kind are coextensive with such identifications.

This in no way takes away the possibilities in such a framework of living a joyous, full, rich existence filled with challenge and mystery, a life of the spirit capable of setting inspiring examples for many.

But for us, engaged here in the examination of all the ways the self can gain more of its prerogatives, conscience is to be considered a trigger of psychic functionings that leave the self less master of its house.

Since there cannot be duty in man without conscience, if we want to return to our self its rights, we must know conscience better.

There are not many schools where we can learn more about conscience than that of the Old Testament and the Talmud and the writings of those inspired by these works.

The very personal God of Abraham, who was prepared to enter into dialogues with Abraham to bargain about punishing sinful people living in Sodom and Gomorrah, is the best knower of how conscience works. He embarks upon educating the tribe of the Hebrews, and through a Covenant, he remains forever the only God of that tribe, and that tribe, the only tribe of that God. The God of Abraham becomes the God of Isaac and later of Jacob too and through him of the twelve tribes, known thereafter by the name of one of them, that of Judah: the Jews (in English). He remains always a personal God, concerned with the minutest interests of the members of that tribe, and teaches behaviors led by conscience, deeply seeped in duty, for every day and every minute. To be an orthodox Jew, today as always, is to conform to the Law, to do only what conscience dictates, the conscience that has been given exclusively to these concrete people and that was made explicit in the commandments and regulations spelled out in the Old Testament.

However much one can find in that remarkable adventure of a few thousand years lived by numerous generations, each generation adding more knowledge of conscience to the other, it remains a fact that only a small fraction of mankind has given itself to knowing even its existence.

Conscience is not the totality of consciousness, and consciousness is only one aspect of the self. Other aspects of consciousness also have the capacity to deal with its kin conscience. In the Bhagavad-Gita Krishna, the God self-endowed with consciousness, gives to Arjuna, in relativistic terms, all the ways available to take care of every one of his involvements that has generated a duty. Arjuna is susceptible to his conscience, and Krishna patiently shows him that, if duty is a lever, then there are duties other than those dictated by one's social, emotional, intellectual involvements. Is one not to attend to one's evolution, to one's self-knowledge, to truth and how truth comes to man?

Duty can also become less dominating if one produces rivals to it and finds oneself divided.

To regain the wholesomeness to which one is entitled because one is human, because one can reach one's self, all that is required to the return to the self. A simple statement but a difficult path, the path of all the yogas (offered to mankind because temperaments make men different), each path perhaps needing more than one life. Once on this path, duty gets lost, and if people become freer because they are more conscious, they are not engaged in the examination of conscience and do not have the preoccupation of knowing more deeply what their duties are, only the discharging of them without fuss and as a matter of course when they come one's way.

In our modern world, man has the benefit of the teachings of all religions and can learn that it is possible (1) to acknowledge conscience as a lever for action to help others, (2) to know conscience as only one aspect of the self, (3) to blend conscience and love and go beyond the living that is directed by a society's laws, and (4) to involve oneself in an evolution that broadens consciousness and, with it, conscience, thereby creating a hierarchy of duties for the person, while the levels of living become such that the duties in them move from the next of kin to the real kin, mankind.

If now we truly want to become freer from our duties, we have a secular approach, which not only does not require that we belong to any established church but also enables us to take advantage of what mankind's experience has been in the realm of religion.

What is required first is accepting with no fuss that one's lot is what it is—finding oneself in a certain place at a certain time, having to cater to so and so, in such conditions and circumstances, and giving enough of oneself to contribute what one can, so long as that does not exhaust the possibilities by the self of knowing more and more of itself. Such acceptance is one of the components of the freeing process; no fuss is a testimony that the self is at the helm, for when the psyche reigns, acrimony at giving to others what one would want for oneself is as sure a concomitant of the discharge of one's duty as is one's attachment to one's gifts of oneself.

By remaining close to how one discharges one's duties, one has available the guidance of truth and can know that a request is correct or that the asker is trespassing. In either case, the response will be the right one. For if one gives what is required, the evidence is there to confirm one's sight of the truth; and if one refuses to give what is asked, one is not going to feel guilty because one is actually being of real help to the trespasser.

This guidance of truth occurs from moment to moment and makes one's responses here and now adaptable to Reality, curbing one's dedication to principle or tradition. Because of this guidance one knows the presence of freedom and feels freer and freer while remaining in contact with the duties stemming from one's place.

One's conscience, illumined by a self that does not lose sight of truth, will bring the tranquility that always accompanies the doing of what is truly right and never accompanies the acts of trespassers, however they feel thwarted by life.

Because duty is a psychic movement, we may find ourselves taking upon ourselves duties that satisfy our ego, duties that enhance our image, duties that have nothing to do with others except in our mind and in the entangled psychic constructs that fool our self.

Thus, we may enter a walk of life that leads us to seek those we want to "serve" and perhaps even to "save," without asking whether by so doing we become trespassers ourselves.

Reading the prophets in the Bible, we meet those who, enlightened by what they call revelation, go out to explain themselves to their people and ask to be understood as speaking in the name of God, of conscience. Because the social context can lend historic truth to a vision, the people may listen and understand. The prophet has no power, but the listeners may give him the power of a seer and give him the right to call them to duty. If they find that what he tells them makes sense in terms of freedom, that is, in terms of using their own will, they change their behavior and find that the world also changes. Insofar as there is agreement between the seer's vision and the content evoked in the people, the seer gets his following. The people acknowledge him as a guide to a better life; he acknowledges the good foundation of his sense of duty and the good inspiration he received in order to give himself to these involvements.

But true prophets are few and far between. Missionaries of all kinds, on the contrary, abound. However well inspired, their characteristic is that they look at others as needing to be helped, improved, and as capable of being helped simply by contact with the missionaries and their messages. This produces in the missionaries a sense of duty which is of the psyche, though paradoxically it is believed to be of the spirit: it is of the psyche because the missionary does not stop to examine what his actions and activities really mean and enters upon them certain that the a priori motives are ample justification for his intervention. Occasionally some missionaries do receive a feedback that wakes them up to the reality of others, but on the whole, the movements of missionaries are centrifugal and concerned only with duties given to themselves by themselves.

Their stories can illustrate, if need be, why it is important to educate in each of us the sense of becoming freer and freer of duty. If we are watchful of the work of the psyche, we discover the propensity to give ourselves to the task of changing others but not to changing our selves, although because these others will come in contact with us as much as we shall come in contact with them, we may have a chance to find how one becomes freer from duty—that is, from the duty taken on by us for any one of many reasons but certainly not because of a certainty that we know the others well enough to involve them in our choice of giving ourselves a priori to our abstract mission.

There are less adventurous people who also want to make others into their own images. They become teachers when they seek a career, they become parents when children happen to them, they become judges when appointed. Duty fills their thoughts and creates the imperatives. They ask for obedience because they feel that it is the duty of the others to obey them, not because they really know the consequences of their actions. The duty of others to obey, which such people take for granted, does not generate in them the duty to know but only the duty to impose. It is such duty that we must learn to examine and to change the sense that goes with it.

We all need to spend some time being in contact with the extension of the sense of duty that emerges from our place in the universe, and see if such extension is something other than the psychic movements that gratify our ego and if it operates at the expense of others.

When the self is in command, duty can be tackled by the self as can all other human moves. But it escapes us when the psyche fools the self. Once more self-awareness alone can free us.

9 From One's Loved Ones

Who can think of becoming freer from those one loves?

As early as my seventh year I became aware that to love means to take on enormous commitments. This I accepted as inevitable for at least ten more years and learned the hard way that such commitment entered upon spontaneously, without any consultation, gives us a taste of the world as a jail.

I was the eighth child in a family in which my widowed mother had the burden and the slight help of nine children. I still see how moved I was by the feeling of her pain at being left behind with so much to do and with so little apparent preparation for it. At first I could give her only attention, affection, and promises that when I grew up things would be different for her and my unmarried sisters. Later I took more and more of her duties that could be passed on to me, like going to the market, preparing breakfast, doing as much myself as was possible, mainly living modestly, not asking for anything beyond the essentials.

I cannot say that she or anyone else in the family knew that inwardly I was so devoted to them. I would wait outside the blankets on cold nights until my brother, four years older, was ready to go to bed so that I could warm him up, as we shared a bed. It did not occur to me that perhaps I could do that inside the blankets, warming his place for him. He never considered my moves as extraordinary, although no one else did it for anyone else in a household where others shared beds.

For years my horizons did not go far beyond our large family and the many relatives spanning three generations, including over fifty young people who visited frequently and played many games in groups. My life was functional—my environment, experiencing the usual events, birth, weddings, diseases, death, celebrating them ritually and traditionally—except for the events of my inner, secret life.

When in adolescence I devoted myself to my affective life, when I became conscious of my love and my capacity to love, I noted that I was the one who endowed everyone with qualities and properties that perhaps they did not care for.

I discovered love-attachment and its ravages.

I discovered that I gave myself rights over others because I loved them or told myself that I loved them.

The shock of this discovery lasted for years, and its echoes are still perceptible in me.

I had refused to use what my father had left me in his will, giving it instead to my unmarried sisters; I gave my mother all my earnings, making sure I had no needs like those of others my age, who smoked, drank, went to dances, visited prostitutes, and thought of a good life as being full of pleasures.

The righteous young man that I was believed that he could extend his protection to others and could ask in return for "decent" behaviors. The cynical people laughed at me. The gullible ones may have acquiesced and made me believe they shared my strict morals.

Soon I found that love was an excuse for the justification of my psychic movements, that in fact I had to become particularly watchful of the fooling that went with love.

In writing this, I know I am using the first person singular and probably distorting the challenge. Nevertheless, over the years, through observation and by proxy, through literature and spoken tales, I have found confirmation that it is important for all of us to be watchful of the fooling that love can and often does represent.

When we love, we relax watchfulness; we associate love and trust, and we give way easily instead of noting the reality behind our observations.

When we love, we indulge in the interpretation of the positive feeling that goes with it, as if this feeling were the sign that we are in contact with truth. Love is called blind, in the popular saying; the loved ones are in a special category, they can do no harm.

But in fact they are no different from others, except in that we have given them our love and not offered it to others.

We magnify what touches us and our beloved ones; we justify our biases and our refusal to gather evidence from events by the movement that puts the loved ones in front and puts everything else out of focus; we then see only what we construct and operate mentally on insufficient evidence as if it were complete and decisive.

Nothing seems as difficult and as painful as to see our beloved ones for what they are. That is why we have the problem of learning to be freer and freer of the loved ones.

Two quite different components belong to this challenge.

One is in an actual move away from the actual loved ones. The other is to understand how the psyche is capable of following the self through love and a number of the psyche's functionings.

The second component may perhaps help in meeting the first, although it has been the other way around in my own life.

We do not understand love by saying it is a feeling; we do not penetrate its mystery by experiencing it. We have to dedicate ourselves to understanding it if we want a chance to come close to its reality.

Love is a movement of the self that begins within each of us. It becomes conscious around adolescence when the self devotes itself to knowing its affectivity.

Then the multiple discoveries that are needed to form love take place.

First, there is the awareness of the free energy of the self, energy capable of generating what did not exist before. The self's movement away from or towards the objectified, which brings out the fact that the self can walk out of old involvements and get into new ones, will make affectivity known as an aspect of the self that is linked with both the future and the objectified. Some energy is withdrawn from previous involvements and made available to the self (which also has its original free energy). It is then that the self knows consciously that residual energy can move from the psyche to affectivity, from entertaining the past to entertaining the future.

Second, there is such immense interest in oneself as a dynamic system capable of so many new functions that the self is overwhelmed meeting them all at once. It becomes confused, hesitant, daring, and timid at the same time, plunged into the new and held back by the momentum of the past. Slowly the past takes its place, becomes instrumental, and more and more the self finds itself engaged in exploring the unknown that reveals itself. The involvements of affectivity are passed on to the psyche once they are sanctioned as proper and functional.

Third, in this dynamic, a clearer feeling of the will and its work takes place, and the notion of a person makes its appearance. The world, until then mainly animated by oneself, becomes inhabited by a few persons, those friends who are like ourselves, while the older schematic approach continues for the rest of the people we encounter. To know a person is by itself so revolutionary that it occupies one's consciousness and makes possible the movement away from egocentricity. It is precisely in this experience that each of us can burst the boundaries of individuality and generate the affective condensation and expansion we recognize from then on and call love.

Fourth, the energy movements known to the self in that state permit the self to acknowledge that there is space within ourselves for at least one other, not as a schema, not as an image, but as a living presence, endowed with will, affectivity, thoughts all his or her own. When that spiritual duality of a space and a person is experienced, we know a longing, and we move towards making one fill the other. The longing becomes a guide for, a forerunner of love, and makes falling in love possible—even if it is with the wrong person or with a person who cannot relate to the space available! Longing as a mood of the self indicates a spiritual space or spaces looking for the person or persons who can be integrated spiritually in the self.

Longing is not a psychic move: first because it aims at an encounter not yet actualized; then because the self is present, actively endowing the search for another with an alertness that makes possible the recognition of the signs that will achieve the matching. But as a move of the self, longing can come into contact with other dynamics, and can slowly merge with the psyche, which makes one long for past states and situations, mixing greed and longing, reducing love to some investment or some commitment where the persons get lost.

The self can keep longing as its light in the expansion of itself in relationships; it can also relegate longing to the psyche, to be free to engage itself somewhere else. It can even make longing become its main movement, and give its conscious life to broadening the range of those who can be integrated into one's self, to universal love, to the love of the whole of nature or creation, with the Creator.

We need to become freer from those loved ones that we have moved from the level of persons to obligations and for whom we no longer feel any longing. We know them psychically as loved ones because memories linger, but we also know intimately that somewhere in the course of living we have let them become creatures of our psyche. We have let them lose the power of inspiring a longing for them. When this happens, relationships have changed from free encounters of selves that know each other as being loved to forced relationships between those who suffer the momentum of having loved.

We cannot meet those loved ones who no longer can inspire as they did, and all the glamorizing that the psyche can do cannot cover the truth that longing is no longer there.

The touchstone of freedom in love, the touchstone that tells us that it is a real couple that has been formed, one that transcends each individual and makes each person be because of the other, is the presence of the longing for the other one, the "missing" one from the individual's viewpoint.

As soon as it is known to either that the couple is a schema, as soon as the longing simply disappears or is replaced by other feelings clearly different (and often the opposite), the loved ones can be a burden, and the self sees that its freedom lies in removing its involvement, if not itself. If no feeling antagonistic to a person is generated, if that person is remembered as a loved one, the freeing may be gradual and possibly successfully achieved. In such a situation, every day one finds oneself freer from that loved one with no ill feeling nor desire to return to earlier states.

It is this move, achieved by so many, that tells us that it is possible to become free of those who had been loved ones while keeping part of oneself engaged in fulfilling social and legal obligations. Being free from love is a paradox only for those who leave the realm of actuality for the realm of abstractions and see love as supernatural rather than human. Love takes place in selves, and like all other phenomena in the self depends on its being and workings. If the self has on all occasions done everything right, has at every moment known all that needed to be known, then it will not make mistakes and will not have to undo the done, to take steps to free itself from former moves.

The complexity of love relationships and the complexities of the selves make the variety of the resulting scene resemble what we meet in life. Infatuation, sympathy, attraction, lust, boredom, can all contribute to placing a neat flow of unreality into the reality that we know; to replacing human relations by games similar to those of one's childhood when partners cooperated happily.

In fact, we all enter into love relations with ease, not knowing that they are among the most complex, the most demanding. To keep persons alive within oneself asks for sensitivity, vulnerability, dedication, attention every minute, readiness to change, to forgive, to be forgiven, to start all over again, to restrain oneself from judgment, from inference, from suspicion, and a lot more.

No wonder, therefore, that not so many love relations reach the apex, the duration, the duality of those loves we read or hear about, that remain true loves for as long as the members of the couple last.

For most human beings to keep up with the demands of love is a challenge whose magnitude is defeating when the demands are taken seriously. Since we do not have an education for love other than the haphazard one that life brings to each of us, we become involved with loved ones not knowing that we have done so—more often than not at the cost of our freedom.

To face this situation we can entertain an education for love that matches the best of all educations, leading towards freedom through correct knowledge, if it is made available. An education for love based on knowledge means only an education based on experience. This is given randomly to all of us, with some of us learning what it really means but most not.

If the experience were to be organized, would it keep alive the correct levers such as longing, or would it produce schemas—dry, hollow schemas—where throbbing life is needed?

Would an education stressing the inner life, the movements of the self, the importance of longing, make us all more cautious in our movements to meet our longing for others and reduce the chances that we take on loved ones who one day become burdens?

In the present state of affairs, we face the problem of enabling those who experience this burden to learn how they can look at themselves and encounter the self in its love involvements in such a way that the freedom of the self is not equivalent to neglect of, or cruelty toward, or cutting oneself off from the loved ones. Since we do not have an education for love, we have to consider the re-education of those who find the loved ones invading, inconsiderate, self-centered as they simply go about their life, in compatibility with their individuality.

Such re-education could be for love or to learn how to escape the consequences of being in the bondage of one's loved ones. The latter requires as well that we maintain social and economic ties while we make our self available for other encounters.

The former may consist of developing an alertness to be set into operation every time longing knocks at the door. This alertness must be followed by a vigilance that recognizes the move of the cohort of psychic substitutes for love, which rush in to comfort or apparently fulfill. Restraint in engaging oneself will be needed. Then a self capable of looking at its own moves critically may provide the caution and the genuineness that will separate love from infatuation and encourage the first while holding in check the second.

For a re-education we need to be prepared to fall in love but not repeat the errors of the past, generally personal errors, caused by ourselves and not the others. We shall be free to the extent we know how to use our watchfulness.

10 From Asking for Anything

This may be my own propensity, but I know that I had to free myself from asking for anything. And in such a book as this, I must give this issue some space.

The message came clearly to me as an injunction from my self, although at the time I did not use this language and probably had not formed the concept. The words were: "Men must ask for nothing."

It could not have been my psyche that reached this conclusion, for I knew that the first word did not apply to the category of human beings, that it was the word for that evolved person who has reached consciousness and lives at a level of awareness that makes life transparent. These Men would not ask.

It was clearly not a psychic movement for the additional reason that the statement became resonant and imperative just as I became aware that I had been given so much, that my life seemed filled with gifts, precious gifts not yet exploited, and that the future could be a feast for me.

The austerity behind the words gained immediate significance, although the total message was understood only slowly over the years.

I accepted it at once as an expression of truth, of the truth of a really spiritual life outside religion. It was to guide me in freeing myself of many of the intricate bonds my psyche had produced. It appeared more and more as a fundamental insight in life, as a powerful rule that could enable me to do in one life what I might have taken several to accomplish in my evolution.

Fifty years later I can see it as a very good example of the working of the self to check the working of the psyche, at least in my case.

The impact of the statement made me sometimes stress "men," sometimes "must," sometimes "ask for," sometimes "nothing."

"Men!" Who were "Men?" Was I one? Were there any humans I knew of who would qualify? Could we become Men if we were not?

My search led me to the view that in our evolution we would understand ourselves better if we inserted a new category of people, the "pre-humans." To define that category I found that I needed to call by this term all those who were asking to become and be different from what they were. It implied no debasing of ourselves to find ourselves pre-human, any more than we are debased when children are called children. It was only a less visible temporal station in the course of evolution of each of us;

that as adults we could remain pre-human while the rotation of the Earth takes us beyond childhood into adulthood.

To become Men, pre-humans had to do something with themselves.

This was not required by life on Earth but was undertaken only if one had been touched by the challenge and moved to find out.

Perhaps by slowly starving all the moves of the psyche, which manifest themselves in illegitimate requests upon life, one could slowly move out of pre-humanity into humanity and start afresh a life in which the immediate adjustment to what life brings and offers is the proper characteristic.

So it appeared dimly that the most worthwhile engagement was one of a continuous state of alertness that would keep me informed of the slightest moves in my inner life and that in this way I could know where I was, what I was doing concretely in the solicitation of events, inner and outer, every day.

The discipline came easily through the examination of the unrolling of time as it took place in its various meanings: content of experience; processes involved; emotions present; the impact of past, present, future; the presence or absence of expectations, investments, and calculations.

Once I found that I simultaneously could live and study life without loss of zest, of genuineness, of authenticity, of total dedication to the task at hand, I could not let myself be fooled by asking to be a Man without first being on the road to becoming one.

In this process, I perceived that life was bigger than any one person, that I could not for a moment take myself to be at its helm, that my place in the cosmos was insignificant, and that the correct attitude towards life was one of surrender. This illumined the meaning of "ask for."

I recognized that I had no business in asking for anything, for it implied that I did not understand my place in the ocean of ignorance and mystery where I, like all others, find myself by virtue of my human condition. Surrender to life is the only reasonable attitude in these circumstances. The rest is illusion, and the jolts and surprises of every day would awake us were we not fooled by the psyche.

Indeed, because our psyche is residual energy engaged in the contact with the past within our individual soma, it can come to the conclusion that the known reigns, that there is security in the stability of the somatic equilibrium, that the closed system of the psyche-cum-soma is all there is. When this view obtains the future has no right to be itself; it becomes the locus of projected wishes and desires, the froth of the psyche functioning in conjunction with the imagination. Pre-humans live the life of the psyche and do not truly engage in a dialogue with the unknown. Hence, the pre-human future is mere extrapolation, is mortgaged in advance. "Ask for" seems permissible because it is no different from living outside true consciousness, and means living in the unrolling of days that are best if they are like happy yesterdays.

Men, by contrast, are only in consciousness, and they know human living as the making explicit of what it is to be aware of oneself in the circumstances of one's life, throughout the day, every day.

In consciousness, unable to invest, unable to mortgage the future, they meet the complexity of every moment with no move towards reduction, simplification, or elimination of what cannot be coped with. This active surrender to life takes care of the impositions of the psyche and the way it works in pre-humans. The surrender carries with it the awareness that one can lead a true life and meet what comes. From this are excluded all the entanglements met in the various chapters above and a lot more as well.

For instance, there is no imposition of logic created by minds to account for the mechanical side of life. There is no "scientific method" beyond letting each problem educate the investigator. There is no supremacy of analysis over other ways of looking at reality. Thought is generated by the self as the substitute for what it knows, in terms that permit, with economy of time and energy, the explicitation of one's intuitions.

Intuition, as a way of being in awareness, means that the self knows that it is holding the whole with all its complexities and is lighting up this or that to the extent one can and for as long as one goes on. Knowing some reality, then, is becoming aware of the relief formed by the successive lightings on the whole. Each knowing is revisable because the lightings are what they are and produce a relief which is not the whole. Each knowing carries with it the knowledge that more can be known, and respects the mystery that the whole, still unknown, can supply.

Intuition is a way of working of Men, and it contrasts sharply with the "methods" used by pre-humans ready to fragment, ready to lose the contact with the whole and to draw useless conclusions about the whole from what little they have deliberately left in the fragments.

Intuition is the way of working of him who does not ask for anything, the way to meet what requires it. By contrast, an understanding of what can produce this or that is not concerned with knowing what is and uses the whole only to force it to deliver an a priori. Pre-humans take away from themselves their chance of knowing the truth about themselves. They can be inebriated by their success until unexpectedly, from behind, they find that their triumphs were misdeeds. The events of the last thirty years on our planet tell us to what extent the planet has been put in danger by the moves of pre-humans refusing contact with the whole.

Freeing oneself from asking for anything is one of the ways each of us has to pass from pre-humanity to humanity. The motivation for willing this shift cannot be reward, for motivation is caused by surrender to truth, and in the here and now this is acknowledged by the self, which is the knower in each of us—the knower of all the truth about us because of its contacts with all its objectivations, all its functionings, and the future.

For Men errors exist only as signs of lack of mastery in the realm of skills and of learning. They do not reflect upon the self, which does not know failure or success, which moves only to grasp the unknown, to let the unknown in, to affect the known. Finally, each individual physiognomy will emerge as only a sample of what is possible for the human conditions in our cosmos. The model of the completed being is not of this realm.

Hence, Men know that to move beyond the threshold of pre-humanity is to enter a universe yet to be charted, one that will extend over the future and provide opportunities for human living outside the old symbolisms that have served pre-humanity, outside the norms and realities constructed for pre-human living which takes place mainly outside consciousness. Men are free from asking, but they do not cease to live. They will use their freed energy in the exploration of the possibilities of human living and conscious living, its new form.

The change is not in the appearances, and no one may see it, but the differences are so many in the way one encounters what comes that even a film of one's life will display behaviors that are not known to pre-humanity.

The pre-human's confusion about himself will make him want to become human, a prehuman move, defeating itself. The transformation from pre-human to human cannot be wanted, but can be willed. For the process consists in stopping oneself from falling into the already trodden paths and is particularly successful if one discovers what it is really to give up wanting and to receive what comes instead.

This is the meaning I see today of the message: "Men must ask for nothing." To become human is concomitant with having reached such contact with oneself that while asking for nothing, one lives a full life, giving every minute to removing the obstacles that prevent one from meeting what is, what comes, because one is alive to everything in the cosmos, on Earth.

Freeing oneself form all psychic moves that involve us more and more in pre-human living, the task we have attempted to study in the previous chapters, will not be sufficient to produce a human life. It seems that the surrender to life is required, which is a move ahead rather than a move away, and the discipline for it does not result from a re-education. Somehow the self must come back to the center of one's life, hearing a call from itself in a moment of inspiration, and must remain at the center to watch the moves of the usurpers within, hidden in the bushes of automatic functionings. Vigilance and watchfulness are needed; the will is needed. But each and all of these in themselves are not enough. One has to know the self as expressing the will to the utmost by surrendering the will in a total move that proves one's intuition of truth and one's place in the universe.

The monologues of the pre-human are then replaced by the dialogues of Man.

Part II

On Making Others Become Freer

Preliminary Remarks

The following few chapters differ from the preceding ones only in that the author is less conspicuous in his presence through the personal pronoun "I." Reverting to a style used in my preceding work, I shall be able to converse with the readers via the subject studied. On the whole it has been possible to treat the subjects of these four chapters as if contemplated from a certain distance; this approach was deliberately avoided in the earlier chapters.

As an educator I have met day in day out challenges closely related to what was happening in the world events that affected people in all sorts of ways. I have let them teach me that all of us have to wake up to all sorts of circumstances and impacts to become more responsive to life and then more responsible with respect to what we find that needs our participation to express its reality.

In choosing what to consider for a book of this kind, I graded for myself the awarenesses that appear to me to have been the most helpful when I have had occasion to relate to others who consulted me. The content of Chapter 11 is the most fundamental since it provides the frame of reference for all the others and for much more. Knowing one's place seems to me so important that I see it as the cornerstone of everyone's re-education and the future of everyone's education.

The subsequent three chapters could have been put in any order and still make as much sense. That absolutes are treated before fears and dependence may also express a bias of mine that puts consciousness before biology. Is it not easier to handle the obstacles presented by the movement of the self and the psyche than it is to handle matters that have biological foundations, such as fears?

Dependence is what I want to reduce, and can reduce, in all my students, for I am aware of its paralyzing effects. Therefore I close this book with a chapter that has educational consequences for all ages and subjects, and is addressed to lay people as well as professionals. Its considerations are linked with the general theme of becoming freer, as studied in all chapters of this book, but they can stand on their own because of their relevance to public education wherever it takes place.

11 From Not Knowing One's Place

One of the hardest challenges we all find is to establish exactly what is our place in the cosmos, in our community, and in the lives of those we live with. On the whole, we exaggerate it in one of two directions, making it too great or too small. Still, it is very important to know it, and every one of us one day or another asks the questions: "What is it?" There are a few principles that may help. The most important is that *if everything (or everybody) has a place, it cannot have the whole place.*

The value of this principle in terms of everyday living is that we shall neither deny a place in our lives to people who want a place or whom we want to have a place, nor deny ourselves the right to a breathing space.

Applied systematically this principle helps us to restore balances in the delicate allocation of places in our lives and of ourselves in the lives of others. Parents are very important, but should not have all the importance an exaggerated devotion may give them.

Work is very important, but should not become everything. Love is very important, but there are other things in the world that also claim our attention. Knowledge is very important, but one can exaggerate its importance and forget that it may become obsolete, that it may be forgotten, and that there is always more coming, and so on.

If we learn to ask the questions, "What is the place of this in life?" and "What place do I have in this or that?" and apply them daily until we get answers pinpointed to the level of here and now, the benefits that result from knowing one's place begin to accumulate and the questions begin to accompany our acts in life and to provide their moderating effect on exaggerated leanings. Knowing one's place, and the grounds on which we can say that we have or must have a place in this or that, or say that this has or must have place in my life, then becomes a device that resolves the generation of much misery for ourselves and others. It permits us to be open to receive while at the same time gives us a chance of not losing ourselves in the gift of ourselves.

A second important principle *is that we are not at the helm of life*. This apparently negative statement is so blatantly true that it may seem ridiculous to mention it; yet very few people display awareness of it, and so many act as if they were.

Observing this principle makes us see things from the point of view of persons who are "carried around" rather than "in charge," even though one may be a chief executive and wield enormous power. For the ship we are to travel on has invisible captains, and we need "luck," "good fortune," "a set of every favorable circumstance" to reach one of our many ports of call. To forget the role of luck in our everyday life is as naive as to believe that only luck is needed. But even if luck is very helpful, it is only one of the invisible captains, and there is a job for each of the crew in all circumstances.

To know that we are not at the helm gives us the humility needed to cope with our immense ignorance, which is inevitable and irreducible, however learned we may be.

Once we manage to live deeply touched by this awareness, we know our own insignificance in front of all the possible happenings on Earth. Though we may work at not being vulnerable and at reducing our sensitivities, we cannot prevent the events caused by cosmic laws either at the planetary scale or at any scale, including the microscopic. Our intellect swells with pride at all the scientific and technological progress of the last few centuries on Earth, but it is also capable of being touched by all that has escaped serious notice so far. Our intellect can help us know that knowledge makes no dent in our ignorance and to realize that we are like corks, liable to find ourselves tossed about anywhere.

Thus, in the universe as a whole, our significance cannot come from our being in charge but rather, despite all our powerlessness, from the fact that there are things we can personally do for ourselves and for others that meet with our approval and/or theirs.

The unending procession of generations through time, one after the other, tells us that each one disappears, that they are remembered because of the good will of those who keep the memory of them alive and not because of the belief that one's position leaves an indelible mark. The great and humble alike are corks, and both may rightly believe they have made a valuable contribution to human evolution. This may be true without implying that only upon reaching the helm can we really contribute what is to be counted on our behalf.

If we follow these two principles by making them part of our daily awareness, we know already that we shall be less jolted, less surprised by what comes our way, and more free to live truth as it manifests itself in our life.

A third principle of some importance is that *none of us can occupy the place of another*. This statement is true provided we acknowledge the uniqueness of each of us.

It is obvious that we will defeat our search for our own singular place if we think of ourselves only as members of a class—Americans, whites, men. In such categories members are by definition equivalent to one another; that is why the proviso above must be considered. Our uniqueness does not come from our individuality (although this is a logical prerequisite) as this or that kind of person. Our uniqueness, as a human property, comes from what we have done with ourselves so that no one can mistake us for anyone else.

The awareness that none of us can occupy the place of another comes when we learn to look at people (including ourselves) outside of all homogenizing properties: sex, nationality, class, profession, age, color, etc. Then we relate to the person in those who come our way, and we shall note the differences, the idiosyncrasies, the peculiarities, and stress these because they make people more interesting. Then the human universe will be so rich in possibilities that we shall have no doubt that we all have a place under the sun. We shall also know that it is our place not the place, and certainly not the top spot everywhere.

I can think of nothing more baffling in this context than the large numbers of so many apparently useless people. If utility were the criterion for being alive, only a few among us would qualify. For most people know their social life as one of fending for themselves and competing for shortages of all sorts. But if the criterion is that we need the whole of humanity in order to live the whole man, then each one of us will qualify for a place and those with the most difficult lives the more so. Hence "monsters" who manage to survive will evoke in us wonderment rather than pity, and we shall learn much from what they did to compensate for lacks and wants, as compared to a "normal" person. We shall all need all the others to bring home to us what it is to be human.

Therefore, each of us may turn to looking at himself or herself and, finding what is one's own, arrive at the conclusion, "Nobody can have me unless I am taken with what I have and for what I am, though I may have only one eye or one arm, be short and slim, snore or wake up slowly in the mornings, be old and weak," and so on. Keeping away from comparisons and competition, we may gather enough insight into the properties of people, disregarding social qualifiers, to discover that indeed we do have access to uniqueness as a human value. In this way, we may be enriched while we obtain acceptance of ourself in our environment.

So, not only can we know that we have a unique place for ourself in the universe, we can also know that everyone has his or her place, a unique complex of relationships with people and things. Some people may find our kind of wit what they like, others our calm or our incredible egocentricity or our capacity to tell fibs or any group of apparently mutually exclusive properties.

The key to knowing one's place is, first, not wanting to be someone else and, then, setting oneself on the way to finding answers to a number of questions about oneself.

Do I want to be accepted through an idea I have of myself? Or just be myself and see who will be moved to become a companion, a friend, a partner, or a lifelong consort?

If I want to be accepted, is it possible to be satisfied by and to pursue the idea of myself? Clearly, to be satisfied is equivalent to not wanting to know my place, not to be interested in finding out what life is when one is oneself.

Do I want to be accepted as someone who knows what is best for myself even when my (miserable) life proves that I am in the dark? Do I know that much of my activity during waking hours consists of being distracted by what takes me away from knowing who I am and what my "correct" place in the world is? What do I do during the day? Am I particularly sensitive to my ego functionings? Or am I surprised by what I hear about myself? Or do I love to be flattered and hate to be seen not so flatteringly? Is my knowledge of my place, as others see it, offensive to my idea of my place, though I still know that I do not know my place?

Does this refusal to acknowledge that I do not know my place and to accept that I should know it complicate matters unnecessarily and make my life still harder?

I may have to find my place again and again, first because it cannot be the same with all, and second because relationships change with time and our place in others' lives changes accordingly.

Do I do what is necessary to show my awareness of these changes?

Do I know that being egocentric is a major obstacle to finding my place anywhere? Or is egocentricity the place where one is sure of one's place?

Do I know that wanting permanence in relationship denies the reality of relationship and replaces it with rigid contracts? Does this not affect my knowing my place?

Is it not true that it is impossible to meet all eventualities in life and that laws become obsolete or need recasting because new facts have come to light? Do I learn from this that permanence is an idea that does not meet with reality? Do I see that if permanence is not a proper end for relationship, it follows that continuous renewal is required for those involved?

If this renewal cannot be generated, one has no clear understanding of why one's place is changing. Since awareness can help one take steps, one has the choice of attempting either to accept the changed place or to renew oneself so as to claim a new place—producing an altered permanence.

Maybe what we must all do more of to know our place at every moment is to give ourselves to understanding the meaning of time. While it is obvious that the rotation of the Earth generates days, seasons, and years, it is quite mysterious how it creates age—that is, that every day is a new day to a changed person. Permanence is the concept that tends to reduce to nothing the flow of time, whose function is everywhere the generation of change.

To know oneself in time is the only true and, therefore, safe place. I am going to change *necessarily*. Only because I am in time am I going to be myself, only when my self in time is aware of this will I live as someone who knows it.

Hence, in childhood one lives like a child, not preoccupied with the unknown future, except with its being unknown.

As an adolescent one lives the changes in the inner life so as to know change and transformation more and more precisely and more and more instrumentally.

As an adult one uncovers the illusory impression that change has come to an end and that one is set on a stable course until retirement and death.

The only continuous thread linking all the moments in our life is the presence of the self, which blends its permanence and its transformations through objectivation, the maintenance of functionings, and constant adaptation to what comes.

Hence, it is open to each of us to stress at the same time both the changes and the self, and to find that our place in time is the foundation of all other awarenesses of our various places in the cosmos and in relationships.

There are, therefore, two ways of improving one's concept of one's place. The first consists in the exercises given earlier of actually working on each challenge as it presents itself and learning more and more to know oneself in relationship. This may require years, and indeed it offers an accelerated growth in the awareness of oneself in the world because of the cumulative effect of awareness and learning.

The other way of improving one's concept of one's place consists of converting oneself from being a study of all and anything that comes one's way to being really clear about what it is to be in time. This second approach, once achieved, will encompass the first and, in addition, will reveal to us our reality. To know oneself in time enhances the here and now while providing a flowing background to all events.

While knowing oneself in time permits the entry, in a more thorough way, into what is required to know one's place, it does not insure that one will look into this challenge. There are many other concomitants worth exploring, and the study of one's place is a special challenge of which not all of us have been made aware. Still, the awareness of oneself in time is extremely valuable, for as life is in time, time presents the encounters. The giving of time to the challenges makes all the difference in our position in life.

It is along this line that maximum help will be found, and we would rather see people select this approach than the less systematic one through which we are randomly affected by whatever comes our way. Answering early enough the question of one's place in the world is one of the most liberating experiences we can provide for ourselves, but to do it while we reach the knowledge of ourselves in time is a much more important move towards realizing our potential in humanity.

To be happy in any routine denies our humanity; to seek routines and be set in them, still more. In fact, to look for security in routine jobs is a pre-human behavior that shrinks away from becoming aware that there is question about one's place. There is no security in life, nor can there be in routines. It is easy to document a statement that much misery in pre-human lives comes from people feeling the jolts and surprises of life as negative, instead of welcoming them as events capable of waking them up to their reality. The contents of the jolts are part of life, the jolts result from our being out of touch with life. Surprises presuppose that we live only the predictable, which in no way describes our constant contact with the unknown. Those who are clear that this contact is our lot are already greatly helped on their way to becoming free from not knowing their place.

12 From Absolutes

Generating absolutes is a functioning of the mind; it consists of adding one mental movement to other mental movements—that of considering these movements as unrevisable and eternal.

Yet as generation follows upon generation, absolutes are pulled down from their status as eternal truths, many to vanish altogether.

Once we are certain that we understand how absolutes are constructed by the mind and that they cannot otherwise exist, our task of freeing ourselves from them becomes much easier. This does not mean, however, that we do not have to work hard at liberating ourselves.

In fact, because of a strange propensity of the mind to propose absolutes to itself, we start the process of generating absolutes very early and fill our psyches with them. The longer we wait to look into them, the more readily they appear as untouchable and as natural.

For instance, because of the wide distance between the physical energy of a strong man and a little child, the latter easily imagines that the strength of men is almost infinite and links to them his awe for that power—until adolescence, that is, when the distance is reduced and often reversed. For years children see their parents as absolutely strong and are very disappointed when they discover that they have made a mistake. Sometimes they use this disappointment to punish themselves and their parents through abuse or even by running away.

The process of generating absolutes is used much more generally than this example can suggest, and only alert people can watch the working of their minds sufficiently to find when absolutes appear and how to recognize their role in life.

It is strange to see in history that so many situations lead to absolutes that have no real basis. We all know of absolute rulers: emperors, kings, and presidents. We also know examples of such rulers being brought down by assassins, coups, and revolutions. But we do not eradicate in ourselves the movements that make us still believe that absolutism is an answer to political crises.

The history of the Roman Church is paved with the suggestion that absolutes are the way to hold the faithful to the right path.

The U. S. Declaration of Independence, the preamble to the French Constitution, consider some intuitions as absolutes, although these intuitions had never been mentioned earlier by governments and had emerged only recently as the awarenesses of certain men.

Thus, the movement that creates absolutes is deeply ingrained not only in an individual's life but in collectivities as well. The need for absolutes may come about when the self, which is in time, loses contact with this need and thoughtlessly attaches itself to the attribute of permanence. Life could teach everyone immediately that since all is in flux, since everything changes, it must be a dysfunction of the mind that seeks to associate attributes like immutability, permanence, identity, to what actually varies, is fleeting, looks different in various lightings.

The self in each of us has only to remain in time to account for our integrity, and our memory of our identity, which is recognizable despite all changes. This acknowledgment of our integrity does not contradict our being in time. An evolving individual gives himself the means to note simultaneously what exists here and now and what is present of the past and of the future in his awareness. Therefore, there is no present which is not accompanied by elements of the past and of the future as well. This confluence of elements generates the continuity often mistaken for permanence, and it similarly generates absolutes, recognizable as such by the self that constructs them—and that, indeed, may need them to cope with the pressures within, to have something to hang onto.

A true man of faith does not feel the need to prove the existence of God. He does not think of God as absolute or otherwise, and hence absolutes are not components of his mental make-up. He does not argue, debate, or discuss, but only lives by faith what is given him.

But a thinking person, submitted to several processes that generate contents, will be concerned with his mental constructs and exaggerate some aspects at the expense of truth.

For instance, it is clear that transformations form a backbone of all that is in time. Without the concept of transformation we cannot understand survival, let alone evolution. Still, the ordinary contact with transformation leads thinking people to stress and give reality to invariants rather than to the transformations. For example, "conservation" is a special kind of invariant production, one that we may be the wiser to leave aside as a true movement of the self. But so many have accepted it as a rallying call, that "conservation" has become a key to much relational thinking. In fact, "conservation," if it were a true movement of the self, would stop our thinking, our personal thinking, from the start. We need, on the contrary, to free ourselves, as babies do, of all investments that structure reality with no reference to truth.

Transformations are one of the powerful ways by which our mind generates more and more awareness of Reality and keeps revealing more of oneself to oneself.

Once we become attuned to looking at transformations rather than at invariants, at what we are becoming rather than at what we cannot remain, at evolution rather than at a static universe that exists only in whoever creates it in his mind, we can answer for ourselves whether or not there are absolutes.

A proper contact with oneself may result in a total relativity of our human universe. Just such relativity was required in the exact sciences, where observations include the observers and where we want to understand what each of us meets as a response to the probes we place in the universe.

Total relativity is a freeing movement because of its truth.

What it actually means is that from the place which is ours we look at our world so that we see what can be revealed of it according to our instruments. For each of us, the world is what we can manage to let be revealed to us. And in our multiple dialogues throughout our lives, we probe differently and at different depths and end up with a collection of grasps, which are as much representative of our temperament, circumstances, education, place, and levels of awareness as of Reality.

In fact, Reality at each instant is the sum total of all these grasps and does not extend beyond what the most advanced observers have made plain. Reality is as much a function of time as are our lives and our works. It does not contain a single absolute besides the postulated ones, which are known as postulates by those who offer them (and which mean little to others, even when they assert them).

Going through life, those of us who remain alert and awake see that the vision of the universe postulated as existing and as extending beyond what anyone can grasp, is changeable and, we say, evolving. This only means that as time goes on and as we become more and more able to ask more and more questions, the questions differ in extent, depth, and content, but are not more important, relevant, to the point, exciting or true than earlier ones. The observer in each of us, from conception to full maturity and death, remains an observer, although with the changing instruments the domain of research is changing.

Instead of talking of absolutes, we can use the valid notion of stressing. Each period of our life, while concerned with a vast number of correlated activities, appears to bring forth a preference for certain kinds of presence while leaving aside others that later will become the center of attention.

During the intrauterine life, the stress is on the making of the soma, the objectified functioning structures of the self. While this goes on, the rest—what will become important soon—is ignored. The objectivations of the self require that the soma be present before it can be used, and therefore it may seem that the soma is an absolute for every fetus, who needs to be entirely taken up in making it.

After birth, the concentration first on the vegetative adaptation to the new environment for a few weeks seems again to exist as an absolute, for again the self needs to be entirely taken up by this adaptation. But because the sensory nerves soon will be at work and the stress will move to perceiving the world, oneself, and the dynamics between both, the former would-be absolute will look much more like a stress on jobs that simply need to be done. Now perception in turn will gain the character of an absolute.

For years boys and girls stress action, and it affects them as if it were an absolute. A closer look shows that shifting from one activity to another, although maintaining the stress on action, provides a universe, with lots of shades, extensions, variations to work on.

A few years later, at adolescence, action being sufficiently surveyed, the self of each of us stresses our inner life with all its infinite variety of emotions, feelings, sentiments. It takes years for a person competent in the fields of perception and action to become as competent in the field of feelings. The emotional life looked at per se during those years again seems to propose affectivity as an absolute. But soon after, for many, the stress on the world of the intellect becomes a new absolute. Reason, thought, and philosophy become the fields of practice for the mind energized by the self.

For many more people, the stress is put on social matters, which in turn apparently becomes an absolute. Most adults remain in that domain for almost all their years. Social dynamics exercise a fascination today that makes most adults see society as an absolute, as untouchable, all powerful, to be obeyed or else.

But beyond society there is the cosmos, humanity, man the creator of cultures and civilizations. Here, too, the stress generates the appearance of absolutes. People seem to perceive only what strikes them and to ignore much that others perceive.

When we take together all the people, either in the world or in some segment of it, we are confronted with many absolutes. Some may conflict with each other. The process of stressing and ignoring cuts layers in the universe, which sometimes makes it impossible for people to know what goes on in a given layer while other people see no more than its contents; yet others see those contents involved with other activities, balancing what happens with what could happen. At the same time, we find that the appearance of absolutes resolves itself in a total relativity, restoring to each the right to be himself, that is, doing now what the stress of the self in some field calls for, enhancing what is being looked at and putting in the shadow what is being ignored.

With such a total relativity at our disposal, we can easily generate in our world the shades and nuances that allow a place in the sun for all of us and all those who will come after us, with the right, of course, of seeing things through their eyes, perceiving the world of their perception, participating in their worlds of feelings and in the social dynamics compatible with their temperament, their intelligence, and their affectivity.

Absolutes are temporary dominants. Temporary can mean as long as one's life if one leaves the absolutes untouched by one's evolution or leaves one's evolution unconcerned with them.

In the ethical world, absolutes (molded like all the others by what one does with oneself) produce special mechanisms in our inner life by generating the movements of guilt, compassion, mercy, forgiveness, indignation, etc., whose functions compel the individual to experience the ties that bind. In this domain more than in other fields of experience, every one wants to know himself or herself as free from some of the feelings and free to act in the case of others.

By bringing people to the realization that they are (1) the makers of absolutes, (2) the ones who adhere to their creation (sometimes justifiably because of the functions of stressing and ignoring, at other times for no valid reason beyond not knowing how to cope with environmental pressures), and (3) the ones who more than once have already thrown themselves wholeheartedly into some field, explored it in the light of the so-called absolute and come out of it in due course—we then can expect that they will meet their actions, their thoughts, their feelings in an atmosphere of relativity. This sense of relativity grows as it is practiced, and soon becomes a tool for managing many behaviors that were unmanageable before.

Tolerance of age, of others, involvements in areas where we are not ourselves, and many more "wise" moves present themselves in order to indicate that we are open, that we understand how others handle themselves and their affairs.

When we meet those who are happily engaged in living some absolute, we know that in their case the investigation of the field defined by that absolute is still going on, and we would easily understand their need for their involvement.

But when we meet those who struggle to get out of some absolute, we have to offer them the instruments of relativity. Intellectually, we may help them acknowledge that it is in their power to move out of involvements as they have done on other occasions. Then we can present them with exercises that bring to their notice the awareness that their present absolutes are made of the same stuff as their previous absolutes—that they are objectivations made by pouring mental energy into molds and, therefore, can be emptied by the withdrawal of energy. This is not an intellectual movement, and the subject must discipline himself or herself to come into contact with the energy within and find out how it operates.

We all know how voluntary muscles respond to orders to act or not act. We all know how to use energy to begin to deliver a speech to any audience or even to one person. We know that the same use of voluntary muscles will also stop us from speaking. On such occasions we can catch ourselves on the threshold of activating the voluntary speech organs, and we have the opportunity to examine its onset, its maintenance, its stoppage. More subtly, we can take a pen and write, while watching how our will sifts, directs, moves all that is needed to form the words, go to the next one, how the arm subordinates to the hand that subordinates to the fingers' more subtle moves, which in turn follow other dynamics in the mind of the writer connected with a flow of words, the structure of the language, the expressions most adequate for the rendering of one's thoughts and impressions.

Mostly because we do not engage in such studies of ourselves, we ignore the energy aspect of life, unless we use the round about way of physics and biology, which altogether leaves aside mental energy and its very subtle movements. But all of us can attain the following:

- entry into the energy aspect of life because we are engaged 24 hours a day in its use,
- contact with the activities while they are taking place,
- growth in the uses of energy and in awareness of its uses,
- growth in the awareness of its transformations,
- closeness with the meanings of energy and what it can do for us.

Every one of us can embark upon being much more knowledgeable about the energy aspect of life and obtain that experience just by being in contact with oneself in activities, every day all day, if one can. Those who need such contact most will find it the hardest to attain, for the initial need results from an original and perhaps continuous neglect of the reality. But contact is possible for some among us, and, therefore, it is possible for all of us, if we all do what the relatively few, so far, do.

In cultures that have developed approaches from outside and believe that such approaches are the only ones valid for knowing, cultures that are more interested in suppressing symptoms than reaching causes and origins, that are organized so as to support research that touches minute matters and refuses to consider broader challenges, we have the extra difficulty that proposals like the above will not be attempted by the people who may most benefit from them.

The most important student of each of us is each of us ourselves, and even technically speaking there is no other way to check exactly what goes on since we cannot remain forever attached to recording machines and no one else would be so foolish as to spend all the time needed with a subject not oneself.

Hence, we have to determine that our problems are better taken care of by ourselves, and embark as soon as possible on the road to acquiring techniques of study that can serve us well. By selecting the realm of absolutes as a field of study, we are less hampered than when we look into fears, as we shall do in the next chapter.

Absolutes being after all temporary and easily known to be temporary and being intellectually more accessible than emotions, we can practice the movement of freeing ourselves of absolutes and end up being free of them, a most valuable contribution to our life, our sanity, and, in particular, to knowing our place.

General relativity is required to understand others and also to understand ourselves. With it, life remains complex and mysterious; without it, absolutes reduce life's complexity sometimes to nothing and, while not eliminating the mystery, make us forget it.

If we need general relativity to make sense of people around us and everywhere, an education for it is required. Until it is more widely offered, we have to give it to ourselves.

Knowing ourselves in that frame of reference will also take care of our inclination to produce absolutes. Their appearance in us will not be opposed, but a vigilant self will let them remain only so long as they perform the functions for which they were proposed and only so long as they are useful to one's self.

13 From Their Fears of Failure

There are fears that are biologically significant, and we all maintain them for what they do for us. For instance, if we are distracted when we cross a road and hear a loud sound that jolts us, we respond immediately by jumping and taking steps as soon as possible to avoid an accident. If a fire starts where we are, we may well have a similar fear that leads us to take steps to avoid being burned. If a ship on the high seas sinks or a plane in the stratosphere is caught in a turmoil, we may feel in either case that our fears are justified. Such fears make our inner state better adapted to the threats in the situation and serve as signals to the self to summon energy and to act.

Fears as such may be looked at as if they denied some human dimension in us. Initially meant to alert us that we were meeting the sudden appearance of an unknown part of the universe, some fears may lose their function and be triggered even when the danger is imaginary. When such responses of our psyche become dominant, our self acts as though it were absent, and we may justly be considered sick (in medical jargon, mentally ill). It is then that we deny ourselves our humanity.

The self engaged in living the present requires concentration, which in turn reduces the preparedness to receive newcomers as it should. From this natural tension, between the self busy at something and the impacts from what is excluded from its awareness, come the responses that can be called fears. They are accompanied by considerable amounts of mobilized residual energy because in meeting the demands of the unknown we are better prepared if we have more energy than too little. The aftermath of fears that do not require the totality of the mobilized energy (which would be needed if, say, we must run away or break through obstacles) takes the forms of trembling and gasping, until the excess energy has settled in its places of reserve.

Fears are healthy so long as the self remains in control.

But there are fears that are constructed by our psyche. People who worry know this etiology well: a routine is upset, and to meet the situation the psyche summons from its storage of possibilities those that represent the greatest mortgage of the future, and it then adheres to them, while other possibilities, which are just as likely, are not retained. Once the possibilities are objectified in the mind, the working of the psyche is triggered, and energy pours into the imagined situation, giving the self the sense of fears at work. These fears could be "justified," and this feeling is sufficient to maintain their presence in one's consciousness. Being slightly aware that the hypotheses have been selected on scant factual grounds, the self may control action but leave to the psyche the display of the dynamics, as if hypotheses were reality, and the situation required mobilization, alertness, concentration.

Entertaining such movements relates temperaments to behaviors, and worriers go on worrying even if their hypotheses are rarely transformed into reality.

But because the process is entirely part of one's inner life, often the self can educate itself to intervene early enough in the process to stop it and to bring the predisposition to worry under control.

Different environments produce different sources of fears: in modern cities we fear criminals, which are not so easily recognizable as are lions or eagles in natural settings; in commercial societies we fear unemployment, which seems to be produced by the blind forces of the economy; in competitive situations we fear failure.

Here we concentrate on the fear of failure.

Spiritually, there is no failure, or, better said, when the self functions as a free agent, it knows here and now only what is. Neither success nor failure are part of that functioning, and only something outside it may generate a frame of reference by which one would distinguish success and failure.

Children know in their play, when it is pure, that they are actively attempting to move towards mastery, and any trial that does not accomplish its aim and then, according to the rules of the game, is rewarded with one's dismissal and replacement by someone else, is judged as validly as a trial that is on target. The player knows only that there will be another opportunity to do better.

When one is engaged at the level of the challenges and is learning, there is certainly more to learn when things don't work than when they work smoothly. Life shows us this truth every day, but we do not take advantage of it every day.

If we apply every day what we know is functional in learning to acquire a skill, we give ourselves a relativistic frame of reference that makes it possible (1) to be in contact with the pure activities in which there is no failure and (2) to know our exact place with respect to the demands of a challenge.

If we experience the fear of failure, we know that we are confronting one of our dysfunctions. We may have left reality and unwittingly entered the area of fantasy. We certainly will not know how to free ourselves from this fear until we reach the functioning and intervene so as to put ourselves into the state required by reality.

Fear of failure is thus squarely put as the responsibility of him who experiences it. The fear exists but not as a necessary feeling, because failure is a construct that is not necessary for meeting the demands of life.

If we enter competitions in which not all can be winners, we know in advance that we may get nothing. If this eventuality affects us before the results are announced, we are clearly indulging in a game where the rules are unreal. If we associate not winning with some personal component that has nothing to do with the activity, we place another unreality in the course of events. We particularly create our own troubles if we begin expecting to win but on no grounds whatsoever. If we fear the outcome in case we do not win, we suffer from a compounded inability to see things as they are.

Although this example has lots of ifs and sounds like a case that hardly ever happens, I see it as a prototype of any number of observations about people entering social competitions, intellectual contests, the stock market, colleges—even marriage and partnerships, where competition is not so obvious.

How many students go to school without any insight about what they are going to do there, who their teachers will be, the significance of what they will give their time to, or what one can do after serving one's time in the classrooms? Still, at the moment of registering for courses, many seem to consider themselves entitled to expect whatever reward there is for those who can satisfy unknown criteria of the college and/or the teacher!

How many people enter into marriage on the basis of their being attracted by someone and of feeling confident that the personal, social, and economic challenges will somehow be met. They rarely are met, and though, statistically, fewer marriages end in separation and divorce than continue, we still do not know enough about what goes on between the spouses and outside of their relationship to allow one to say that a marriage is a success.

How many people visit a physician ignorant of anatomy and physiology, ignorant of what needs to be known in order to make sense of their condition, ignorant of the state of knowledge of their physician? Still, they expect that all these circumstances will somehow take care of themselves so as to produce the results wished for. Medical doctors, for their part, refuse to speak of cure, they know only treatments, and it is these that fail or succeed, not they. Rather, they let people attribute to them successes but refuse to have anything to do with failure. In fact, only their patients experience failure and fear it.

How many people every day trust that elevators, buses, trains, planes, etc., will do their work, although the only things they know about them are that they sometimes (mostly) work and sometimes break down? In all of us, trust holds fear in check, and we go about entering these mechanical objects with no conscious expectation about their functioning, feeling free to think that we shall reach our destination. When they fail, we experience inconvenience and sometimes great danger, but if we survive, we do not lose trust in them because of their failure.

In these few examples, we can see that our condition forces us to be in situations where our ignorance, in spite of its immensity, does not prevent us from living and using only whatever we know; that knowledge and ignorance are complementary. No amount of knowledge can reduce our ignorance, and ignorance has little to do with our knowledge; rather, life presents us with a sense that we are equipped to become aware and to retain what we become aware of in ourselves and, through our brain and our senses (part of our nervous system), the world around, and to discover that there is much that is beyond our awareness.

These conditions of human living need to be explicitly known by all. This knowledge, as an awareness of what it is to be human, will now provide the means for a re-education that will take care of our fear of failure.

We talk of re-education because we are considering here those who already have let such fears establish themselves in their minds and are ready to agree that they have often been subjected to the pressures of fear of failure. Education will come in when it is clear that it is cheaper and more effective than re-education.

In such a re-education, the first milestone will consist of the discovery that the notion that we can distinguish enough of the present and the future to act on the basis of fearing failure and hailing success is only a view of the mind. In fact, what appears as one at this moment (success or failure) may turn out to be the other, and conversely.

The second milestone consists of knowing that when we are engaged in vital activities, there is neither failure nor success, only successive moments, each one teaching us something important in relation to the activity.

The third is to enter into activities always watchful that the outcome not coincide with our expectations, and to make this a rule in our living. We quickly learn that the movement of watchfulness is as easy as the movement of expectation and much safer because it takes the odds into account.

A fourth milestone is that in the economics of energy it is much more profitable to save the amounts that nourish panics and fears and use them for whatever returns they can produce, perhaps for looking at ourselves before we engage in speculative activities.

A fifth will consist of examining the variety of our involvements and determining which of the so-called failures have consequences that can be coped with and which are beyond our strength. Once this inventory is made, we can examine whether we find ourselves attracted by involvements that will lead to an achievement we can live with or by those that will shatter us. Failure will then have a real meaning, and we shall move into the future more knowledgeable about these matters. We shall know our responsibility in the outcome of our actions, and fear will only be an expression of lingering psychic movements, as happens in greed.

If ever we can re-educate ourselves to the point that we can live without expectation but not without drive, without investment but not without commitment, without ambition but not without resolution, without egocentricity but not without presence, we shall know that there cannot be any fear left in us that our actions will let us down. We shall know ourselves as free from the recurrence of the thing we labeled failure, which made us prefer to avoid it rather than face it.

There are movements in us that keep us in unreality. Not knowing which ones they are makes our lives less our own and puts us at the mercy of what could be avoided. The movement we must resist most is the one that simplifies life to such an extent that we see events as coming and going with only two attributes—they touch us, or they do not. Instead, we can educate in ourselves an open vulnerability that shows us the complexity of both ourselves and the universe and at the same time the opportunities for our self to lead a more human life shot through at every moment with all sorts of open possibilities that neither repeat the past nor maintain the status quo but offer to a growing person wider challenges and deeper insights.

By reducing the fear of failure through knowing what generates failure and then how fears follow suit, we give ourselves a great deal more than elbow room: we become more competent of being at the helm of our personal life. This is possible because of the central functions of the self and our awareness that each of us is his or her own self.

14 From Dependence

It seems obvious a priori that because knowledge has been accumulated over the centuries, to acquire it each of us must relate to it as if from a position of inferiority. Those who do not know look up to those who know, until knowledge is passed on (or down) from one to the other, and those who did not know become knowledgeable in turn.

In the Middle Ages the road to the mastery of a craft took years, and the apprentice who was attached to a master generally had a hard time filling the gap between his skill as a clumsy beginner and the skill of his resourceful and smooth master.

School education follows a similar scheme. Through a curriculum sliced into so many years, it presents students with amounts of knowledge that necessitate nine or ten months for assimilation through exercises and homework.

In the case of the apprentice, dependence results not only from the real gap in skill between himself and his master but also from the opportunities provided by the master to examine the functionings of the skillful person and to practice those techniques that are compatible with the apprentice's equipment. A huge gap between master and apprentice is a handicap in the acquisition of a skill; it keeps the apprentice dependent for a longer time than would a narrower gap. In this perspective, it would be more profitable for apprentices not to attach themselves to highly skilled masters and to seek those who may still be finding their feet themselves.

Another source of dependence that the learner frequently experiences is the expectation of perfection. The belief that mistakes must be avoided at all cost goes against the purpose of practice, which assumes the lack of mastery and therefore the possibility of errors. If we want to be realistic, we must accept mistakes as part of learning. It is a component of the freeing movement and a requirement for its implementation.

In schools teachers rarely consider that their job is to make students independent.

First of all, knowledge is usually seen as something external that has to be received and retained. This is also called memorized knowledge. Hence, exercises are given to ensure retention. Drill and repetition have for centuries served that purpose and are still utilized. Scholastic testing is mainly of this function.

Secondly, teachers themselves are rarely independent. Their training has been such that with most subjects they perform at a level far lower than the inventors of the subjects. Their studies insist there is no royal path to knowledge, only hard work and enough exercises. Their contract requires from them only specifically designated gestures in agreement with the curriculum and the regulations set up by the employers.

Thirdly, on the whole, human learning has not been studied until recently, and even now only a handful of scientists know exactly what it is and how to cope with it.

In view of the above facts, then, it is unfair to clamor for a reform in education, which can come only when enough people understand the function of education.

Hence the importance of this discussion for those who want to prepare themselves to help others become <u>independent</u> by becoming independent themselves first.

It has long been known that a true awareness liberates.

All of us have known independence in learning in our early childhood.

We learned on our own to grasp, to turn, to sit, to stand, to walk, and to jump. We learned to look and listen, to discriminate colors, shapes, sizes, sounds, pitches, durations, and intensities, all on our own. We learned to make sounds and adapt them to the sounds produced by people in our environment, and learned to make sense of how language functions, all on our own, using every gift we had that was relevant to the task on hand.*

Still, in spite of all that proven competence, so many among us are incompetent in mathematics, in foreign languages, after years of schooling!

At the root of this incompetence is our dependence, a multiple dependence at that. Because we know that we can forget, we feel dependent on an unreliable memory. We have been made to use outer criteria, such as the approval of teachers, and we have been prevented from developing inner criteria that resemble those that guided us in our early spontaneous learnings. We have been made to let someone either take us by the hand and tell us hew much we should move at every step or else to spoon feed us. We have been submitted to external tests from time to time and made to believe that they were the criteria of our achievement, for the tests gave us the grades, all important for the professionals and through them, society.

Hence, if we want to free people from dependence, we must look into all these components and find whether or not we can substitute for each a functioning that truly leads to independence.

---

* See my study, The Universe of Babies, Educational Solutions, Inc., 1973.

It is clear that whatever information cannot be invented and must be retained (as, for example, vocabulary in a new language) should be entrusted to one's memory.

No one can progress in any area where things have to be remembered without mobilizing part of oneself to hold the remembered items.

I have given the name ogden to this specific process of energy mobilization, to indicate the amount needed for each single memory we can count on. It would cost, for example, ten thousand ogdens to have available ten thousand words in any one language.

Those of us who are teachers must see to it that our students know that unless they "pay their ogdens" for what they cannot invent, they cannot use the needed material. It is a dual responsibility of the teacher and the student, the former to make clear that only paying ogdens (using one's energy to memorize) can solve the problem and the latter to actually pay them.

But of course there is much more to human learning than paying ogdens, and much can be invented by each of us or simply perceived or obtained by transformation from what we already know. From the start, we can provide our students with an awareness that they hold the keys to the functionings and that by becoming aware of what they are doing (1) they learn what there is to learn and (2) they know that they possess inner criteria and that these criteria are the source of the new knowledge. All this is equivalent to being independent as a learner.

In all my pedagogical work, there are hundreds of examples of how this can be done in the basic subjects and in foreign languages. A few will be noted here.

1. In the field of foreign languages I have organized for each language (except Chinese) a colored chart called its "Fidel,"* which displays all the signs for all the sounds of that language, including all the spellings used in that language for various sounds. The colors are selected so that a viewer, comparing the Fidel of his language and that of the new language, sees at once that he does not have to memorize all the sounds of that language because many are already part of his equipment. He sees how many are new and will require payment of ogdens to be retained (and also whether he has to pay ogdens for the script).

Our experimentation over the years has shown that such an exercise (1) saves time, (2) eliminates anxiety and doubt, (3) generates a clear understanding of the task, and (4) makes sense to the student, who sees that reading and writing, uttering and listening, all work together to establish reliable foundations for one's entry into the new language.

---

* Soon after the first edition of this work, a new kind of Fidel was introduced for a number of languages, made only of colored rectangles, thus avoiding the distractions of the script of each language. Now this sound/color chart is an essential instrument to do the work described here.

Because of the inner criteria created by such a survey of the sounds of the new language, the student is at ease with other activities involving these sounds, such as stringing them together to produce words and sentences. These sequences of amalgamated sounds can be acted upon through other powers owned by the students, such as inflection of the voice, pauses and phrasing, and these activities provide the certainty that one's organs of speech are capable of producing spontaneously, and without a model, long statements in the new language that sound remarkably close to those of natives. And for all this the teacher uses only the visible movements of a pointer on the visible signs of the Fidel, in a code of action objectifying time and rhythm.

From such a basis we can take our students to other peaks and other spontaneous performances, which in turn generate enormous confidence that the new language is easy to learn because one is learning so much so quickly. For example, in about one hour for most languages, students can learn to read any numeral of up to 15 digits in the decimal system and, under dictation, can write in figures any number of the digits' names. Numeration, normally an insuperable obstacle for people learning a new language, becomes the first field mastered in this approach. From this mastery the arithmetic one knows in one's language is made available in the new language for the meager investment of the few ogdens it costs to learn to reach the arithmetical signs—for example, +, -, x, , .

These examples indicate, I hope, that it is possible to eliminate dependence upon a teacher even in an area where a priori there is a huge gulf between the students, who know nothing, and the teacher, who knows everything. By concentrating on what makes learners independent, by producing the instruments (in this case, the Fidel and the teacher's pointer) that relieve memory and remain available all the time, and by making students pay the required ogdens and go through specific exercises that practice the material paid for, we free our students of so much that ordinarily would long remain obstacles in their learning.

For the expansion of the approach and the maintenance of the state of independence, a number of other instruments are needed and many exercises with them. Teachers here as in other fields have two responsibilities: one, to force awareness of what is involved in each situation, and two, to provide practice to obtain facility. Awareness and facility are attributes of the students, but they are the job of the teachers. They carry with them the elimination of dependence since the inner criteria that the students create take care of dependence. These criteria bring the evidence that the students are autonomous in the area under study, for they enable students to take initiative on what they mastered as if they were natives and to feel that they can stand by what they do. This is the meaning of being responsible.

Not only do students feel comfortable in the new language, they also enjoy their contact with it because their acquaintance with it is much more than knowledge: they experience a feeling for it, aesthetic as much as intimate, one full of promises.

Such results were totally unexpected in the field and are telling proof that education is ultimately concerned with freeing students and that for this we need to relate to their awareness, the involvement of their self in the creation of new forms that integrate their past. Because the new is compatible with the past, the psyche does not present its usual resistances and lets affectivity play its part, as is revealed by the joy of the students, the relaxation they experience, and their constant progress.

Teaching has blended with education because of the attention paid to the human components in the situation.

Through our experiments with teaching languages in this way, we see clearly that everyone who wishes to can acquire a good working level in at least one language every year—this while studying the other subjects required of our school children.

2. In the field of mathematics, as most people know, the situation is not much better than it is for languages. So many students never develop a liking for the subject, and to almost everyone it neither relates to what they see as their place in the world nor exists as an area in which they can feel active.

Dependence again arises because so much seems linked to memory. So few criteria are available other than the teacher's acceptance of answers, and when answers are rejected, no reason is given except their inexactitude. For example, there does not seem to be any basis for 7x8 to be 56 except the statement in the table of multiplication that says so. If the sum is forgotten, the student, in the beginning, would not know what to do to find it.

But here too it has been possible to find how to give back to all students inner criteria, to reduce to almost nothing the reference to memory, and to develop in students a zest for the activities that produce mathematics.

The basis of all independence is in the realization that what one does is accessible to and can be acted upon by an alert self, the same self that crosses roads and climbs steps. Hence, by discovering that perception and action are the bases of mathematization, we have opened the door to a multitude of activities that can be entered upon at once and can yield mathematics immediately.*

In our approach, the chapter of algebra called "arithmetic progressions" has been looked at as the activity of going up some steps and the formalization of this activity. Similarly, we have looked at the odometer in a car, the wheels in clocks, or the meters that record gas and electricity consumption in the home, and we have seen in them "geometric progressions."

We can look at the set of our fingers and see in it "complementary subsets" and "numeration" (in all bases) simply by relating, for the first, to our ability to fold some fingers and stretch the others and, for the second, to our capacity to label the same set in different ways, calling each finger either a unit, or _____ ty, or hundred, and so on.*

---

* A microcomputer program, Visible and Tangible Math, has since 1982 made available for home study and schools our proposals.

But however impressive the yields from such modest beginnings, they are little compared to the awareness that "transformations" are the backbone of "equivalences" and that these, by their nature, make the world of relationship look very full and varied and capable of indefinite renewal. This affective tone is no exaggeration of ours; each student's self is brought into contact with the tremendous power of lighting the same wholes again and again and always getting at once some new insight.

Students can see that if only one educated one's sight and looked at relationships, this approach would yield what was invisible. For instance, if a is recognized to be equal to 7 x b, then at the same time b must be recognized as 1/7 x a.

Every relationship applies to infinities of entities recognizable as related to each other but still different, giving the notion of equivalence so much more power than identity or equality, the preferred definition in the schools. For example, "twice" is a relationship between elements of pairs, which in the case of integers alone produces the infinity: 2~2x1, 4~2x2, 6~2x3, and so on, where 2x is read "twice" and ~ as "is equivalent to." Read in reverse, such relationship produces the following infinity of pairs: 1~1/2x2, 2~1/2x4, 3~1/2x6, etc., defining the relationship "one half."

The pairs linked by "one half" can serve as an example to illustrate the mathematical mode of thought, in which the stressing and ignoring process becomes a fount of entities. 2/4 and 3/6 look different; their names are different. But both are equivalent expressions for 1/2 and hence for each other.

It is by introducing students to this elementary, even primitive, use of their mind that we free them from the anxiety created by holding in oneself what one does not comprehend while requiring that it remains intact. Now we can systematically use the process of "stressing this and ignoring that" to produce cascades of labels for the same contemplated universe. By making awareness the object of our attention, we can let students see that to do mathematics is as simple as: "if you can say a, you can say aa," and let them encounter this in as many fields as is needed to give them the facility required.

For our readers to be closer to such thought, it will be sufficient to let them think how the addition of 1 produces all the integers, how doubling repeated from 1 generates exponentials, how finding the midpoint of a segment is sufficient to prove that that segment has an infinity of points, and so on.

The awareness that it is always possible to act upon the given via certain transformations compatible with it, and to let the awareness take a form in which one's mind reads at once what there is to see, is an awareness that reveals to everyone how the creative mathematician works. As an extremely elementary illustration, we can consider a subtraction such as 10,213 - 8,769 (which we take 3 years to teach in elementary schools). In the past, the given could not be touched, and a procedure, introduced only once to cover all cases, had to be used to find the answer. Today, we see the given subtraction as a member of an infinite class of equivalent differences, the simplest being n-o (o being zero and n the "classical" answer). To find n we can see the given of 10,213 - 8,769 as (10,000 - 8,769) + 213; the bracket is one of the names of the complement of 8,769 in 10,000 or 1,231. Hence n is 1,444 and is obtained by adding 213 to the complement. Every subtraction appears as an addition on a complement, and this looks very different from what was originally given.

Mathematics is a universe that is always growing, and always needs to be recast by those who inhabit it. Our students can be invited to share this kind of life from the beginning of their study. We no longer need to burden their memory with many isolated relationships, but can ask them to look and tell us what they see. Teacher and student together verbalize what is encountered, call it by the prestigious name of "theorem," and even give to it a student's proper name, as if it had been found for the first time (Stephen's theorem). Such practice will make students see that to do mathematics, although it is a special type of activity, is not necessarily the activity of specialists. The simple awareness that everyone can enter this field—a fact too long hidden from most people—had not been reached earlier because not enough people had studied what it is to do mathematics. Now we not only have that awareness, we also know how to invite all students to mathematical banquets where they can take as much as their appetite permits and feel satisfied (if they don't give themselves indigestion!).

There is no need now for anyone to miss the enormous excitement that accompanies the revelations our mind brings to itself when contemplating intellectually the dynamic infinities that are always present in any mathematical situation. The treatment of all mathematical questions can be such that, from the start, the main impact on the mind of each student comes from the deliberate insertion of infinite classes in what each contemplates. The "one" we need to "add to itself" to make two, the "one" we need to add to two to make three, etc., requires a bag containing an infinity of "ones," all identical to each other and minted by the same machine. As soon as "two" is made, we need also an infinity of these, and so on. Such bags of integers make much more sense to teachers and students alike than the single "one" of logicians and mathematicians.

Because of the wealth that students feel with such an approach, they will not hesitate to be generous, even spendthrifts. Operations will form sets, families and classes; will be iterated, combined, made to act upon "objects" of the mind; will transform situations. Students will feel they can take some steps of their own, original, authentic, controlled. Hence, independence will pay; autonomy and responsibility will follow.

Imagery belongs to the dynamics of the mind; algebra and geometry will affect each other through images. Perception of properties in sets of configurations will again lead to theorems, which are simply expressions of awareness. Proofs will be used to convince others that what one sees is truly like that. Rigor is the result of demanding dialogues between the one who wants to convince and the one who does not let himself be easily swayed.

As all this indicates, we are far from the classical attitude to mathematics that made so many people sure that not only did they waste their time in its study, but also that they were not cut out for it. The majestic edifice transmitted by tradition was too imposing, too intimidating, it could lead for most only to a feeling of inadequacy and of total dependence on others. A human outlook is found by looking at mathematization rather than mathematics, at the activity of minds, those of mathematicians, and seeing them as they often are—fumbling, hesitating, abandoning some attempts, trying others, then accepting for itself, and not as the ultimate word, the results they have found.

Mathematicians were babies and children who gained their title only through dedication to certain kinds of uses of themselves. It is precisely this that can help educators give back to each child his right to know accurately whether he wishes to dedicate himself to this activity or prefers another for his own reasons.

Only free people have such choices.

Although we have treated the two examples of language and mathematics at length, they are only sketches of the actual working that takes days, weeks, and even months. During all these days, teachers and students go through inner evolutions that represent their true education. To know a new language or some mathematics may be useful in social living, but to have come across oneself as a dynamic mind capable of doing now, as in early childhood, the "right things" and meeting challenges for what they are, is far more important. From the utilitarian point of view, one can see that what was possible once will be possible again; from the spiritual point of view, one finds that one knows one's place in learning, a place from which it becomes clear that we all take part in the generation of knowledge, that the outer and inner worlds are intertwined, and that our world makes a place for each of us just as it is partly made by us.

The freedom of knowing our place in the learning process adds itself to the freedom produced from all the other movements looked at earlier. The awarenesses (1) that learning is so much broader than memorizing what we are told to remember; (2) that learning is an active process for the learner, who thus participates in the production of the unique fabric of his consciousness; and (3) that learning assists in one's overall evolution, and, in particular, the illumination of some relationships of the self and the non-self, all this will contribute to making each of us more of a person, more oneself, and, because of this, will contribute to collective evolution.

Dependence has been seen here from the false perspective that we need others when we can be independent and need only ourselves. The achievement of some independence is equivalent to the disappearance of some dependence. Of course, since we are not everybody at the same time, we shall encounter all the time what others have generated and we cannot invent, and on these occasions we shall meet ourselves as dependent. But we shall also know that it is a transitory state which can be replaced by independence if we pay the price, first in ogdens, in order to own what we cannot produce by ourselves, and then in dedication, to become functional in that area.

Freedom in learning will be sensed as the inner movements that constantly reduce the weight of what is not ours by the presence of our own creations, creations that use the powers of our self and its capacity to objectify and to dwell in the objectivations. Freedom will be felt when the psyche and the brain take over the automated functionings that free the self to forge ahead, to consider literature in the field of language, for example, or applied mathematics in the field of mathematics.

Elsewhere we have worked on other areas in which man is a learner, and every time our proposals have been designed to free students deliberately from dependence and aim at autonomous and responsible learners. By using what each student brings to the task and by being acquainted with how one learns what is implicit in skills and capabilities, we can help others become freer of inhibitions, of anxiety, of all the hampering moves, and at the same time we can enable them to experience an expansion of their self in the new universe open to them. This kind of teaching belongs to the theme of this book.

As to the other kinds of dependence that we all know about, they will not be treated here separately.

But let us say this about them:

1 that the progress made on meeting all the subjects treated may be sufficient to provide a way of handling other dependences;

2 that some dependences may well have been the adequate responses at the time, and in such cases,

moving away from dependence could be the job for a freer self or must be found somewhere other than where the dependence operates;

3 that the actual practices of freedom have not been worked out in this text, only how to become freer. Hence, when we need to transfer what was learned in one area to another one, we assume that the freer person we have become will know not only that some pressures have diminished in some sectors of our life but also that change has occurred because we are a freer person. Only when this second awareness is at work will we manage transfers as a whole and in every area of living;

4 that dependence can be a necessity and then needs to be accepted as a matter of course, as in the case of crippled people and those who attend to them.

Dependence can be of affectivity, as well as of the psyche, and it can be put in contact with independence and propose its problems to the self.

The self, acknowledging dependence, can find that it is genuine and that nothing can be done about it, and can make the psyche consent not to evoke nostalgia for the time when one was, say, not bedridden or impoverished or old. This peace, this quiet, generated by the self in conjunction with the psyche, is as useful as becoming independent.

In our Earthian, human condition we are all bound to a soma, and we all find ways to use that dependence to generate all the independences compatible with it. We lose our humanness if we want to deny our somatic dependence. When we reach a close contact with it, we feel freer in that we do not from then on attempt to act as if we were in another condition.

In Part I we studied a number of examples of dependence on movements of the psyche and how we became freer when it was clear that we had to and could. In this chapter, we have considered briefly two examples that make us see how, when we have studied a phenomenon that concerns dependence, we can offer means of fostering independence instead. Whenever this is possible, it will give us other examples of what could have been included under the heading of this chapter.

Further Readings

Introduction a la psychologie de l'affectivite. 1952. Translated into English, French, Portuguese, Spanish.

Un nouveau phenomene psychosomatique. 1952.

Teaching Mathematics to Deaf Children. 1958.

For the Teaching of Mathematics, vol. 1, 2, 3. 1962-64. Vol. 4 and 5 in preparation.

A Scientific Study of the Problem of Reading. 1962. Second edition 1968.

Teaching Foreign Languages in Schools The Silent Way. 1963. Second edition 1972.

Towards a Visual Culture. 1969. Translated into French, German, Spanish.

What We Owe Children. 1970 & 1971. Translated into French and German.

The Universe of Babies. 1973. Translated into Japanese, 1988.

An Experimental School. 1973.

The Common Sense of Teaching Mathematics. 1974.

The Common Sense of Teaching Foreign Languages. 1976.

The Common Sense of Teaching Reading and Writing. 1985.

Of Boys and Girls. 1975.

The Mind Teaches the Brain. 1975.

The Science of Education (Part 1). 1987.

Teaching and Learning Foreign Languages. 1985.

Know Your Children as They Are, A Book for Parents. 1988.

* * *

In the field of literacy we have managed through the microcomputer to offer students activities which make them independent, autonomous and responsible in an unbelievably short time. These programs come under the name of Infused Reading and exist for a few languages using Latin characters.

www.ingramcontent.com/pod-product-compliance
Lightning Source LLC
LaVergne TN
LVHW061221100826
845148LV00004B/824
9780878250851